The Concept of Community: Lessons from the Bronx

Harold DeRienzo

IPOC
www.ipocpress.com

Harold DeRienzo

Copyright © 2008 IPOC di Pietro Condemi Milan Italy
All rights reserved. No part of this publication may be reproduced, distributed, or transmitted in any form or by any means, including photocopying, recording, or other electronic or mechanical methods, without the prior written permission of the publisher, except in the case of brief quotations embodied in critical reviews and certain other noncommercial uses permitted by copyright law. For permission requests, write to the publisher at the address below:

IPOC di Pietro Condemi
8, Via Albricci
I - 20122 Milano
Ph.: +39-0236569954
Fax.: +39-0236569954
ipoc@ipocpress.com

Printed in the United States and the United Kingdom on acid-free paper

ISBN: 978-88-95145-18-1

Front cover: Elena Carlini, *Walldrawing*, 2005 www.mtartegallery.com

Contents

	Acknowledgements	9
	Preface	13
I	"Over-Identification": My Introduction to Community Development	21
II	A Community Development Primer	45
III	Working Concepts and Definitions	67
IV	Community and Neighborhood: Toward a Transformative Model	75
V	Empowerment	91
VI	Politics and Democracy	97
VII	Culture and Multi-Culturalism	109
VIII	Social Capital	117
IX	Community Organizing	123
X	Bias, Prejudice, and Racism	139
XI	Economics and the Inner City Community	151
XII	Public Policy	169
XIII	The Importance of Place	197
XIV	Banana Kelly Revisited	211
XV	The Loss of Community and the Loss of Democracy	221
	Bibliography	237

The Concept of Community

To all those who struggle, and never lose faith.

Acknowledgements

I have always believed that a firm sense of self, loving relationships, and a stable personal life are the necessary preconditions to any success. So first let me acknowledge my parents, Harold, Sr. and Catherine DeRienzo, my wife, Helena Fields-DeRienzo, and my children, Christopher, Chantel, and KoySean.

I have also been blessed with friends and colleagues who have partnered with me in projects that to any outsider must have appeared daunting. In my early years of community work, Larry Savage, Larry Klein, Hector Montes and others provided me with important guidance and support. Later, while I was working at Banana Kelly, outside supporters such as Meyer Parodneck, Martin Young, Ron Shiffman, Phillip St. Georges, Ramon Rueda, Robert Nazario and Cheryl Edmonds provided me with technical back-up, working examples of what was "possible," and moral support.

My local partners, Leon Potts, Robert and Hopey Foster, Gloria and Eric Wingate, Armando Martinez, Steve and Quentin Dickerson, Mildred Velez, James David, "Buckey," Melissa Goldsmith and others stood united, maintaining resolve in spite of local resistance, ridicule, and even violent confrontation. Frank Potts, without whom no amount of successful organizing on Kelly Street would have been possible, always was available to add perspective, wisdom and guidance to our local efforts.

In the eighties and nineties, I was blessed by colleagues who provided criticism and lessons that were outside my own experience. Sandra Colon introduced me to organizing techniques and philosophies that formed the basis for much of my most successful work in the field. Susan Saegert's infusion of environmental psychology into community development work opened my mind to new dimensions and new techniques for designing community programs. Michele Cotton, as piercing and annoying as her always-on-target critiques could be, never shied from pushing me to test my assumptions, clarify my goals, and communicate my intentions. Bonnie Brower, with her quick tongue and sardonic wit, taught me that there is no compromise when it comes to right and wrong.

Throughout my thirty years in the field, Fernando "Freddy" Ferrer has been a consistent partner, friend, and counselor. Richard Kahan taught me how to combine local talent with outside professional assistance to arrive at sound and defensible public policy positions. Eddie Bautista constantly demonstrated that having fun while doing difficult work is both important and appropriate. Marcy Benstock never stopped reminding me that vigilance must be constant and that no victory is permanent. Karolyn Gould helped me enhance my own sense of how morality is a critical component of our work. Barry Milberg never hesitated to help rescue a struggling group or get a new group on its feet. And I would also like to thank Ron Shiffman, who painstakingly reviewed this book and helped fill in gaps that either pre-date by involvement in the field or were outside of my experience. I also appreciate his gracious acceptance for often being used in this book as a foil in order to make, or elaborate on, a point.

My colleagues at the Parodneck Foundation and CATCH, along with the support I have enjoyed over the years from their boards of directors, have provided me with great flexibility and space within which to explore new avenues for development and best practices. Working alongside truly dedicated and committed people makes community development a pleasure. I thank Thomasina White for her humanity and her dedication; Dalila Morales for never giving up and always making me smile; Amanda Garcia-Reyes for helping to keep me honest; Marcia Evans for her passion; Carlton Collier for never being satisfied that we have accomplished enough, and Eugenia Flatow for always being there as a colleague and a friend. I am also grateful to John DiMatteo for help received through his Milan office of Wilkie, Farr & Gallagher, L.L.P.

Finally, I thank my editor, Catherine Hiller, who took a 500-page manuscript and helped turn it into readable book. Her professionalism, patience and unselfish guidance were critical to this book's completion. I also thank her for serving as my "cognitive barometer" and in the process ensuring that this book is accessible to more than a handful of professionals and academics and is helpful to all community developers.

Preface

I first moved to Fox Street in the South Bronx in 1976. It was a bad year for the Big Apple. The City of New York was on the verge of bankruptcy. Infamously, the Ford Administration declined to help, leading to the headline in the *New York Daily News* "Ford to City: Drop Dead." The state was poised to place the city in receivership. Things were even worse in the South Bronx, where arson led to the abandonment of whole neighborhoods. New York City's housing administrator proposed a planning policy for the South Bronx and other economically marginal areas that was immediately characterized as "planned shrinkage."

Soon, the fires and mayhem in the South Bronx would be widely known through daily news reports about fleeing residents and confused city officials; through stark visuals and commentary delivered by the sportscaster Howard Cossell during the 1977 World Series; and through the later film, *Fort Apache The Bronx* (which was wildly biased in its racial stereotyping of local residents). This was the context for my introduction into the then-emerging field of community development.

College Volunteer. At the time, I was a college graduate working afternoons and evenings on Simpson Street at the Casita Maria Settlement House. It was a tough job for many reasons, including the fact that my supervisor insisted that I apply 1950's style "group work" techniques in working with the youth of the area. The idea behind group work was that organizing groups of youngsters around collective activities would provide a substitute and preclude the need for joining street gangs. From my experience, it was like putting the proverbial band-aid on a cancer. While I organized ping-pong tournaments, Halloween parties and cooking classes for pre-teens and teens, the homes of these youngsters were burning down. I remember a brother and a sister who were doing very poorly in school. I arranged for tutoring help in English and Math, as well as daily homework help. But when I made a home visit, I learned that their family had been burned out of separate homes no less than three times in the past year! No wonder the children were having trouble in school.

I decided to spend my free time working with residents on the issue that seemed most relevant to them: saving their homes. While in college, I had volunteered as a tenant and community organizer for the newly-formed Northwest Bronx Community and Clergy Coalition. I was trained in "Alinsky-style" organizing techniques, techniques that focused strategic organizing tactics, such as rent strikes, demonstrations, and media exposure, targeted against identifiable "enemies." However, it did not take long to realize that these techniques were about as outdated as the group work techniques I had employed at the Settlement House.

Depopulation. Besides the problem of organizing tenants against vanishing or non-existent landlords and an economically crippled local government, I was organizing a constantly diminishing resident base. As quickly as I organized tenants, they moved away to other, seemingly safer, areas of the South Bronx – primarily to areas around the Grand Concourse. Fires are violent, frightening and deadly events made all the more terrifying when they become daily occurrences. During this time, many South Bronx children (such as my youngest stepson) went to bed with a set of street clothes under their blankets in case they had to flee in the night.

Most of the fires were caused by arson sponsored by owners or their agents and carried out by local residents. Most had the good grace to slip notes under the apartment doors in the buildings scheduled for torching. "Be out by 9 PM!"

warned one note shown to me. Similar notes had been deposited under each door of a building on Simpson Street. And that, along with word-of-mouth, was considered to be sufficient warning. Some residents would return to their apartments after the fires. It was not uncommon to see someone living on the fifth or sixth floor of a burned-out building hauling water from a fire hydrant up a pulley affixed to the fire escape or roof. As the buildings became increasingly abandoned by both landlords and tenants, anti-social elements in the area would move in and set up impromptu social clubs on the first floors. When the initial group of volunteers at Banana Kelly began to clean out 940 Kelly Street in preparation for a sweat equity project, we set up shop in the former social club on the north side of the first floor. The building was a four-story, eight-unit building with two railroad flats on either side of each floor. On the south side of the first floor was an apartment completely covered with no less than four feet of debris, 90% of which consisted of beer cans. Essentially, the social club functioned on the south side of the building and the north side served as its trash receptacle.

A Hopeless Situation? Under these dire circumstances, nearly everyone with an option to move exercised it. I would visit the families that I had come to know through the children I worked with at the Settlement House in an attempt to organize a response to the explosive circumstances of a neighborhood under siege. Most often I was told by those I was trying to help that the situation was hopeless and beyond the reach of any organized effort. Existing area community groups were of little help. These groups, still funded through varied though diminishing government programs, were either stuck in the past funded glory of the "War on Poverty" programs or committed to a future that required as many large vacant buildings as possible, for the only subsidized rehabilitation program available to local community development groups was the federal Section 8 program, which was used at the time to renovate vacant buildings.

One resident told me that I had no right to suggest that anyone should stay and fight for their homes when I myself lived in a more secure area in another part of the city. Shortly after that encounter, I left the Yorkville section of

Manhattan and moved to Fox Street, about three blocks from Banana Kelly. After I relocated, I made some headway with the people on Barretto Street and Simpson Street, but most of the successes were of a limited scope and duration – except for those on the section of Kelly Street known as "Banana Kelly" on account of its crescent shape. Through the Banana Kelly Community Improvement Association, Inc., my colleagues and I had a comprehensive impact on local residents. Because of its success, and because it was emblematic of work done by similar groups throughout New York City, Banana Kelly has been the subject of books, articles and theses.[1]

It is on Kelly Street that my most intense work in the field of community development started and where I began learning what became a long series of lessons in community development, lessons I have tried to incorporate in this work.

The South Bronx Experience. My original intention in writing this book was to produce a practitioner's guide to community development, with particular emphasis on giving the young, aspiring community developer some theory, background and lessons based upon real experience. As the work developed, my experiences began to overtake the theoretical parts of the text and I decided to go with the flow and simply write an autobiographically-based book. It became an account mostly of community development in the South Bronx from my

---

[1] For example, see Roberta Brandes Gratz, *The Living City: How America's Cities Are Being Revitalized by Thinking Small in a Big Way,* John Wiley, 1994; Maria Sclavi's *La Signora Va Nel Bronx*, written in Italian, La Vespe, 2000, and published in English by IPOC Press, 2007. John Jiler, *Sleeping with the Mayor: A True Story,* Hungry Mind Press, 1997, also devotes more than one chapter to a part of Banana Kelly's history and significance, but unfortunately the author relied entirely on Yolanda Rivera's public relations materials, and the information about Banana Kelly is mostly wrong. In the late seventies, Roberta Gratz convinced the Municipal Art Society, which had never before focused on any preservation efforts outside Manhattan, to devote an entire issue of *The Livable City*, July 1979, to Banana Kelly and similar efforts in the South Bronx. The Regional Plan Association did the same a year later. Over the years, numerous articles about Banana Kelly appeared in the New York Daily News, the New York Post, the Wall Street Journal, and the New York Times, among others. The U.S New and World Report reported on Banana Kelly in its issue of June 1, 1981, pp. 23-24.

perspective. This perspective comes from thirty years in the field and many leadership roles: as advocate, organizer, researcher, lawyer, mediator, developer, financial intermediary, broker, technical assistance provider, troubleshooter, and lender. I have built alliances with local residents and seen the power that comes from giving people the tools and space to develop their own agenda and further their collective interests. But I have also seen this power used against the very people whose interest they were designed to advance. I have engaged in many productive alliances with government officials. But at times, I have failed to recognize masked political objectives that became apparent later on.

I have worked with many banks and other lending institutions, creating programs that were models for the city and nation. The most recent of these was the first program to provide relief to senior citizen homeowners in New York City who have been victimized by predatory lending practices. But I have also been used by bankers who needed a way to advance a successful audit or get some merger approved. They said they would work to arrange grants and loans beneficial to them and to my organizations. Very often, these verbal promises were broken when they received their approval or an acceptable CRA rating.

This work is not intended to be a handbook for any particular aspect of community development. Rather, this work is intended to provide the reader with the perspective necessary to understand the complexities, intricacies, and contradictions inherent to any comprehensive community development effort. In many sections of the book I raise more questions than I answer. My intention is not to solve the diverse and daunting problems confronting those engaged in community development but to provide a framework and perspective for working in the field. No one person, regardless of his or her experience or success, has the last word on this topic.

A Unique Time Period. All in all, my experiences have been productive, worthwhile, and rewarding. But I had opportunities that may not be available to those who now seek to make a career in community development. I organized a not-for-profit housing and community development corporation when I was twenty-three years of age. Granted, there was a fair degree of risk. I moved into an area of the South Bronx that was burning at an alarming rate. At that time, I was the only white person in the neighborhood, working and living in a cultural environment I found both intriguing and overwhelming.

Unlike activists affiliated with church groups or national organizations, I had no institutional backing. For a while, I lived off the generosity of the good people of Kelly Street until I was able to receive outside funding. In the process of stumbling through the housing protection, preservation and development for others, I personally experienced fires, building collapses, and ridicule. Early members of our group were chided for "working for free for a white man." In fact, on one occasion, while Leon Potts and I were standing next to one another on the east side of Kelly Street, a shot rang out from the building across the street. The bullet grazed Leon's right arm. To this day, we have no idea who fired the shot, which one of us was targeted, or why.

But as difficult as that time was, there were opportunities for anyone with vision, tenacity, patience, and a penchant for hard work. This was the beginning of what was to become known as the community development movement. Areas such as the South Bronx of the seventies provided good training for future leaders, many of whom went on to high level jobs in government and finance. To name just a few: Kathryn Wylde went from working as a community activist in the Sunset Park section of Brooklyn to leading the New York City Partnership (New York City's Chamber of Commerce) and is currently one of the most influential players in New York's real estate development and investment. Gary Hattem, who ran St. Nicholas Preservation Corporation in the Greenpoint area of Brooklyn, went on to become a high level official with Deutsche Bank. Felice Michetti went from running a Bronx neighborhood preservation office of the city's housing department to running the city's Department of Housing Preservation and Development. Today she is President of Grenadier Realty Company, one of the largest private management companies in the world.

Learning Labs. The South Bronx and other inner city areas became learning labs for implementing ideas and creative processes; a proving ground for new ways of doing business. We all made many honest mistakes along the way.

But those mistakes were absorbed because all of those who would become friends and colleagues over the years were willing to put in the work to make up for the missteps.

The opportunity to grow from within the community development sector is no longer available to a similar degree. If a group of residents now takes over an abandoned building, they are not lauded as "urban pioneers," they are branded "squatters" and arrested. Today, no group would be able to take over abandoned buildings (including privately owned buildings) and fashion a construction-training program around their rehabilitation – and eventually convince a government agency to pay the cost, as we did in 1977.

This book is part auto-biographical, part sociological, part philosophical, and part practical. Community development is not a science, but it is a discipline that embraces many of the environmental, behavioral, engineering, and other social sciences. Above all, community development is an exciting field of work because it involves people and the testing of individual and collective human potential in circumstances that are ever-changing and increasingly challenging. Real accomplishment is hard won but very gratifying.

Whither Community? It is important to recognize that today there is a major constraint to community development work, namely, the withering away of community itself. Community is a concept that can connote the best of what the people of this country and the world can accomplish when they work together. But community is in many ways anathema to the prevailing economic, political and social trends.

When I was younger, I believed that it was possible to develop a political framework, and from that political framework would emerge social and civic institutions. In other words, I believed that economics, social organization, institutional development and society derived from the dominant political reality. Now I have come to believe that politics follows from the dominant economy – not the other way around. Our economy is dependent upon a pliant, mobile workforce, so there is little practical tolerance for social organization beyond the individual, the family and church groups. Concomitant with the reorganization of the economy, union membership has declined precipitously. The concept of community, further developed within the body of this work, is not easily reconciled with the dominant economy. On the contrary: our political, social, monetary and other institutional structures have been developed to complement, support, and further sectors of the economy that actually undermine communities.

Nonetheless, I cannot fathom a popular, democratic alternative to community. Community development still remains a vital and noble endeavor. This book is the culmination and continuation of my life's work, offered in the hope that it will enhance the efforts of others to create true community in America.

I "Over-Identification": My Introduction to Community Organizing

In the early seventies, I attended Manhattan College, which is paradoxically located in the North Bronx. The college officially designated its address as "Riverdale, New York." Riverdale was an upscale, socially-detached and formerly-gated community, while the Bronx had rougher connotations.

My college experience was typical for those years. College life revolved around student activity: drugs, alcohol, politics. Advocacy groups demonstrated for the liberal causes of the day, with which I sympathized, and there was little discipline on campus. After 5 pm each day, there was no visible authority at the college. Students generally ran wild. Parties in the resident halls were raucous and ongoing. During the day, classes were held, tests were administered, and diplomas were issued on schedule, but the administration had adopted a siege mentality.

In my sophomore year of college, to my parents' dismay, I decided that accounting would not be my chosen profession. I considered dropping out of school altogether, but that year my number in the draft lottery was dangerously low at 102. If I left school, I would be headed for Vietnam – or to Canada, as a draft-dodger. My longtime girlfriend broke up with me, and I was adrift and searching.

I was looking for something that would tell me how the world worked and expose me to different kinds of people. I wanted to test the prevailing assumptions and "discover the truth." Most importantly, I wanted to do good and meaningful work.

Into the Ghetto. One day I saw a recruitment poster for the "Social Action Group." They were recruiting volunteers for a tutoring program working out of the Casita Maria Settlement House on Simpson Street, in the South Bronx. After hearing a description of the program from SAG's leader, Larry Klein (who remains a good friend to this day), I decided to join the volunteer effort at Casita Maria.

That was my introduction to the "ghetto."

When I first set foot in the South Bronx I was awed. It was an area more densely populated than any I had ever visited. There were people everywhere: in the streets (mostly playing stickball or skelsies – a street game involving bottle caps and chalk), on the sidewalks (talking, arguing, banging on congas, playing dominoes), hanging out of the windows, sitting on the fire escapes and on the roofs (flying kites or flying pigeons). Hallways smelled of garlic-laden *pernil,* and the sounds of salsa pulsed from every corner. The vibrant Puerto Rican culture enthralled me. The language, music, games and food were all novel, while the extraordinary emphasis on family was familiar to me, as an Italian-American.

At the time, the 41st Precinct, later known as "Fort Apache," also had the nation's highest unsolved homicide rate.

Twice a week, a group of us would travel in an ailing red Volkswagen van from Manhattan College to the South Bronx. We'd go south on the Major Deegan Expressway, enter Port Morris, and travel up Bruckner Boulevard to Simpson Street. It was strange to be traveling underneath the Bruckner Expressway, which seemed to have been expressly designed to both by-pass and bury this community. Once at the Settlement House, we volunteers would go upstairs to the classrooms on the second floor to give homework help and tutor the grade-school youngsters.

Settlement Kids. Most of the children were young and eager to learn. They welcomed the chance to supplement their education and receive special attention. One of the first children I worked with was a young boy who was about eleven. The most important thing in his life was his graffiti name. One day in the boys' room at his school, he discovered that someone had "stolen" his name. Although I told him it wasn't important, he was completely committed to finding that person and righting this terrible injustice.

There were other surprises. As an Italian-American, I found kissing and hugging almost second nature. And first I was happily impressed by how much kissing went on between the boys and girls. I saw it as a form of social cohesion and support. After a while, however, I realized that all this kissing was not so benign. Older boys, in their teens would yell out to the younger girls, "Mommie," pointing to their cheeks, and the younger girls would dutifully kiss them in what now appeared as a concession to authority and the corollary social subjugation of the younger females.

I would later see this subjugation operate in the extreme when in the 1980s, at the height of the crack epidemic in the South Bronx, young men in their late teens who were in control of their corners would carry on with much younger teen girls who would ultimately bear the children of dead or imprisoned fathers. I didn't like this social subjugation of the younger females, but I couldn't do much about it, although it did dampen my own enthusiasm for such demonstrations.

One family – the Bonaparte family – was dominant on the block, and at one time or another, I got to tutor most of the members of that extended family. (And yes, the oldest male was named Napoleon, and went by "Napo," for short.) Just as they dominated the 900-block of Simpson Street, they also dominated much of what went on in the Settlement House.

Dominance was necessary for survival in those days. I remember one day in the late Spring when I was at the Settlement House and saw Napo running down the street, obviously being pursued. At one point he stopped a few steps from the Settlement House and I heard him say aloud, "What am I running for?" He was on his block and could depend on his family for protection. No physical confrontation ensued.

Each week, I looked forward to my tutoring sessions. I probably got more out of the experience than many of the youngsters I taught. Many of them, through what they were taught and the esteem-boosting experience of meriting one-on-one attention, went on to excel in their studies. I felt it was a great privilege to be one-on-one and in small groups with some of the most beautiful and energetic children I had ever met.

After Larry graduated, I took over the Social Action Group at Manhattan College. I expanded its activities and its volunteer base and raised money to buy a brand new Dodge van (for $4,000).

Organizing Tenants. In my senior year, I became involved in another local volunteer effort. A joint effort organized by Manhattan College and Fordham University was providing students with training and field work in tenant and community organizing. The group that we were assigned to work with, the newly organized Northwest Bronx Community and Clergy Coalition, was intent upon stopping the "South Bronx," with its violence and fires (and, perhaps, its residents), from spreading any further north. After the course training, I worked as a volunteer on Villa Avenue, one block west of the Grand Concourse, a neighborhood of mostly older residents of European descent. The block was a mix of small houses and multiple dwellings, housing mainly older residents of European descent.

In the classroom we learned about the organizing techniques of Saul Alinsky, the famous depression-era organizer from Chicago who is the father of Community Organizing and who founded the still active and successful Industrial Areas Foundation. In the evenings and weekends, we put the newly learned organizing principles to work, organizing residents around issues of concern, which mostly had to do with neighborhood security. We would often combine our efforts with the student and volunteer organizers from other areas of the Northwest Bronx. Through this experience, I learned three noteworthy lessons.

Three Lessons. Lesson #1: You Never Hold All the Marbles. After much outreach to the residents, we decided that we would put together a community forum on the subject of greatest concern to them all: neighborhood security. We developed our agenda in consultation with a group of resident leaders. Everybody in the group agreed that one particular individual would lead the forum. He was first on the agenda, and the others would follow him.

On the night of the forum, we organizers were excited. Over a hundred residents had turned out. Our first speaker, of the five who planned to speak, went to the front of the room. As it turned out, he was also the last. He had taken it upon himself to invite no less than five of the top brass in the police department, and for two hours one uniformed police official after another droned on, trying to convince those in attendance that all was being taken care of and there was no cause for alarm (or for organizational efforts). After two hours of this, the meeting ended. The forum had been designed to affirm collective resolve and to plan change. Instead, it provided the exact opposite: a debilitating call to rely on the status quo.

Lesson # 2: Outcomes Often Define Themselves. Working with another group of resident leaders, we organized a forum and were able to get Deputy Mayor James Cavanaugh to attend. This forum promised to be a singular opportunity for local resident leaders to confront the Mayor Beame's administration at a high level to express local issues of concern and to elicit a response about how the city would meet the needs of the people. Shortly after the forum began, however, a very loud and angry group of other residents crashed the meeting, turning it into a demonstration. As young organizers, we were crushed. We believed that all of our efforts had been in vain. Rev. Paul Brandt, a Jesuit from Fordham University who was leading our effort, consoled us. He told us to consider what the Deputy Mayor had taken away from the meeting. Perhaps the demonstrators would have a more dramatic and lasting impact upon him than all of the reasoned arguments our group had been prepared to make.

Lesson #3: If You Think You Know, Think Again. In my organizing on Villa Avenue, I was shocked by how many tenants lacked what I considered basic services: front doors that locked, consistent heat and hot water, etc. Consequently, it was puzzling and demoralizing that I was unable to organize tenant associations within the buildings to fight for better services. One day, a kindly older gentleman took me aside. He told me the ridiculously low rent he was paying, and then, with old world courtesy, he told me to get lost. Of course, he would have liked to have had better services, but his astonishingly low rent was much more important to him and to the other tenants than restoration of services.

Through these experiences, I was able to learn while still in college that organizing is dynamic, and in spite of the best strategic planning, outcomes seldom turn out as planned.

I was busy. I still attended classes, wrote papers, crammed for exams. I spent my evenings and weekends shuttling between Simpson Street and Villa Avenue in the Bronx, and Queens Children's Hospital, which was then the children's part of Creedmoor Psychiatric Center.

There, a group of us would spend Saturdays supplementing the recreational activities of youngsters on Thorazine. It was challenging to get them interested in an activity – and when we succeeded, it was difficult and disheartening to bring it to an end.

Casita Maria Full Time. I graduated from Manhattan College in 1975 with a Bachelor of Science in Business Administration. It was the middle of the most severe economic downturn since the depression. The only recruiters for business majors at the Manhattan College campus that year were representatives from insurance companies who hoped to recruit enough seniors to profit from signing their families and friends up for insurance – and to hell with whatever happened next. Luckily, I wasn't interested in working in a mainstream organization anyway, still less in insurance.

Both the Northwest Bronx Community and Clergy Coalition and Casita Maria offered me jobs upon graduation. I decided to work at Casita Maria, partly because one of my supervisors would be another Manhattan College alumnus, Larry Savage (who also remains a friend to this day), and partly because I loved the Puerto Rican vibe.

As a group worker, my hours were from 1 pm to 9 pm. When I arrived each day, I was expected to do paperwork and plan activities. After school let out and the grade-school students arrived, I would use group activities to develop their social skills and inspire their curiosity. We went on trips to museums, roller skating rinks, and parks. Sometimes in bad weather, we would stay in, playing dodge ball or cooking dinner. In good weather, my groups were often involved in organized sports. I was always alert to individual needs, which I would address in private.

Later in the day, I supervised the evening session of the Settlement House, which ran from 6:30 PM to 9:30 PM for the local teen-agers. In the evening session, the Settlement House provided a safe place for teens to socialize and play table tennis, board games and the like. The idea was to promote healthy exposure to rules and boundaries that might, perhaps, translate into more productive interaction outside the Settlement House. If nothing else, Casita Maria's evening session provided young members with a respite from the mean streets of the South Bronx. During the evenings, I coached the basketball team, planned activities with the teenage members – and broke up any fights.

I became engrossed in my job. I would arrive at work very early, sometimes at ten or eleven, and I began to organize trips and activities for the weekends, including sleepovers in the homes of friends from college out of the area or even out of the state. I never felt at risk in the neighborhood because I was literally protected by the families I worked with. In some ways, I became part of the extended family of Simpson Street.

My supervisor at the Settlement House told me that I was "over-identifying" with the local residents. If that is a sin, I am guilty of it to this day.

A Visit to Harlem. Of course, there were tense moments at Casita Maria. One winter evening in 1976, I took my basketball team, our cheerleaders, and other Settlement House members to the Drew Hamilton Houses in Harlem for a basketball game. During the game, as is often the case, the cheerleaders on each side of the gym yelled insults at each other. By the end of the game, the insults became threats.

With the best of intentions, I gathered my group together before we left the projects to give them a little pep talk. I told them that we only had a few blocks' walk to get to the subway station. We would stay together as a group, and everything would be all right.

Yeah, sure.

We did not even make it out of the common area within the projects before we were surrounded by a loud, hostile crowd. I found myself bouncing from – and stopping – one small fight after another. I cursed my own stupidity at not having called the police and asking for an escort to the subway. Soon, onlookers at the windows began throwing bottles at us.

Then a young man drew a knife on one of my group, and I grabbed the knife from him by the blade. The scene was totally absurd. Here I was, a twenty-two-year- old, hippie-like, white-bread social worker, standing in a crowd of at least a hundred Harlem blacks, holding a knife by the blade. Now I was the center of attention. I heard someone say, "Hey, white boy, what are you going to do with that knife?" It must have looked as though a young, suburban-raised idiot was looking to take on a growing crowd with one dull knife -- for even though I clutched it by the blade, I wasn't bleeding.

What could I do? I quickly sought out the oldest-looking member of that crowd – perhaps he was thirty – and simply handed him the knife. Later on, I would learn that at that very moment, a young man approached me from behind with a bat. Just as he was about to clock me, one of my group, a kid named Kenneth Hooks, grabbed the bat from him and threw it. Kenneth probably saved my life.

My kids ran off in different directions, and the crowd scattered in pursuit. Eventually the police did arrive, and I made it to the subway in one piece. But only a few members of my group were at the station. Upon returning to the Settlement House, I spent a good part of the night calling people's homes to make sure all my kids got home safely. Then I went home myself.

Living in the 'Hood. In 1976, I moved into the neighborhood, at 930 Fox Street, a newly renovated, federally-subsidized building, the redevelopment of which was sponsored by Father Gigante's organization, the Southeast Bronx Community Organization, or "SEBCO." The building was just around the corner from Casita Maria, so it was very convenient. Still, I felt quite alone and culturally isolated in the off hours. When I gave up my job at the Settlement House, I was unable to keep my apartment, so I left prior to being evicted, moving first to Vyse Avenue, then to Kelly Street.

For over twenty years, I lived in the South Bronx, and as I went about my daily life, I would often see the kids I had worked with at the Settlement House. Living in the area, making it my home, and personally confronting the challenges of everyday life helped me empathize with my clients and with other families who either refused or were unable to move from an increasingly desperate and violent neighborhood. I think my living in the South Bronx helped the residents trust me. I was not just another do-gooder outsider. Of course, living among them gave me yet another excuse to "over-identify" with my clients. Many were my neighbors, and some became my friends.

Building Fires and Abandonment. The fires were reaching epidemic proportions, and I found myself organizing residents to fight the arson and landlord abandonment. In 1976, the building across from the Settlement House caught on fire. It was a rather large building, with two wings and about 40 units. After the fire was put out, I worked to save the homes of families who lived on the opposite side of the building from the fire. I spoke to my boss, who at the time was the Treasurer of SEBCO. I tried to convince him to find the money to seal up the damaged part of the building, so these families would not have to relocate. No luck. At the time, SEBCO was only interested in vacant buildings for redevelopment – which would enable SEBCO to use the newly created federal Section 8 rehabilitation program. Occupied buildings were apparently not worth the effort.

Later, when I lived on Vyse Avenue, I witnessed an even more egregious effort to accelerate abandonment. At the time, the City was in the midst of its worst-ever fiscal crisis, and in an attempt to collect back real estate taxes and to counter rampant charges about "phantom bookkeeping," the City passed what came to be known as the "quick vesting" law. Under this law, the City was authorized to foreclose and take title to buildings after only one year of tax arrears. In 1978, 1138 Vyse Avenue was taken over by the City. Services became sporadic. Many of the best tenants began to leave, and anti-social elements began to move in. I remember at one time, in an effort to stabilize the building, I physically removed stolen car parts from where they were being stored in the hallway of the building – much to the surprise of the "owners." My efforts were to no avail. Eventually the heat and hot water service went from sporadic to non-existent.

Some years later, we learned from the daughter of the superintendent that he had been paid by a local not-for-profit group to turn off the heat and hot water to get people to move out so the group would qualify for lucrative Section 8 funding from the federal government. The leader of that group, probably for similar reasons, ultimately wound up in jail; the building was eventually demolished, and today is the site of a number of neat row houses, occupied by middle-class residents.

Some of my efforts were more fruitful, but only in those buildings where there was strong, usually female, tenant leadership. One building on Barretto Street, for instance, went on to become one of the city's first tenant cooperatives – from among the thousands of buildings taken over by the city.

Taking a Stand. Some of the adults with whom I worked at Casita Maria asked if they could sometimes use the gym. As it was reserved for teenagers until 9:30, once a week I opened the Settlement House from 9:30 P.M. to midnight to allow local adults to play basketball. After these sessions, we would gather in the gym and the office to drink beer and smoke and talk about ways to stop the fires from consuming the entire neighborhood. Through these talks, I met Leon Potts and other residents from Kelly Street, the curved portion of which is known as "Banana Kelly." We began putting together plans for action. We decided to make a stand on Kelly Street and stop the fires that had already consumed six of the fifteen buildings on the block. And we were largely successful: after that we didn't lose any more buildings on that block.

Between 1970 and 1980, the population of Bronx Community District 2 went from about 100,000 to 30,000 residents. The lively density that had awed me as an undergraduate was replaced by a bleak desolation: block after block of burned out tenements; residents warming themselves at garbage-can fires; abandoned, stripped-down cars; innumerable fires on vacant lots burning electrical cable for the copper within.

Another alumnus of Manhattan College, Hector Montes, coached basketball with me at Casita Maria. At the time, Hector was a "street-banker" for Chemical Bank. His job was to bring in business that would not normally find its own way to Chemical Bank – or to any bank, for that matter.

The Peoples Development Corporation. At the time, Chemical Bank was providing construction loans to so-called "sweat equity" groups. Sweat was their only down payment for loans that would let them live in affordable, cooperatively-owned housing. The groups would create this housing by taking over abandoned buildings and renovating them. Hector arranged for a group from Kelly Street to visit the Peoples Development Corporation (PDC) on Washington Avenue in Morrisania, in one of the buildings they had renovated.

The PDC was actually a group from East Harlem, organized by a local resident, Ramon Rueda. He decided to apply his efforts outside East Harlem because that area already had an established sweat equity group known as the Renegades *[sic]* of East Harlem – "Gang for the People." Ramon was one of the most articulate, charismatic people I have ever met. His group got started by "liberating" a newly renovated building that was 99% completed but, due to contract disputes, was still vacant. They took over that building and went on to squat in numerous other buildings in Morrisania.

When we went to visit, 1178 Washington Avenue was nearly finished, and we witnessed first-hand a beautifully renovated building that had been completed by local residents. Now these people were getting trained and paid to do more rehabilitation work in the neighborhood. My group was very impressed, and we were determined to make this happen across town on Kelly Street.

The Banana Kelly Corporation. The initial excitement lasted for many months, during which we established a corporation, the Banana Kelly Community Improvement Association, Inc., put together a position paper, learned about other groups in the city doing the same work, and found out about the few potential resources available for us.

While in this planning stage, I was offered a job at the East Harlem branch of Casita Maria Settlement House. It was tempting, since my salary would have gone from $8,000 a year to a princely $13,000. But I was well into this new and exciting sweat equity venture, so I declined the job in East Harlem.

Progress at Banana Kelly was slow, and I shared my frustration with Phillip St. Georges, the director of the Urban Homesteading Assistance Board (U-HAB). U-HAB provided technical and training assistance to organized groups of residents who were committed to providing "sweat equity" labor in vacant buildings that would later be run as low-income cooperatives. I hoped that Philip would figure out a way I could work at Banana Kelly full-time, so I could really get it moving. I wanted to spend all my time dealing with what was then the most pressing concern for residents of the South Bronx – the daily fires that were consuming the neighborhood.

Phillip helped me put together an application for the New York State Neighborhood Preservation Program. While we waited to hear the result of our submission, he told me that U-HAB could certainly pay me $100 a week to concentrate on my organizing and development work. I remember him saying that I was doing U-HAB's work anyway, so I deserved a little compensation.

Based upon this commitment, I quit my job at the Settlement House, where I had worked full-time for two years, and began to work full time at Banana Kelly. After two weeks, when it was payday, I went to the U-HAB office. The only person there was Howard Burchman, the Fiscal Director – everyone else was out celebrating their paychecks. I told Howard of Phillip's commitment, and he said that there was no money for me. I left U-HAB dejected and defeated, with one token in my pocket and thirty-five cents to my name.

For several months, things were rather strained. I often relied on the families of Kelly Street to give me meals – rice, beans, pig knuckles, and the like.

Just before being evicted, I vacated my apartment on Fox Street, after which I grew even more dependent on the kindness and generosity of friends.

Still, organizing at Kelly Street was exciting. We attended meetings of the community board, met with other local leaders, passed out position papers, organized street clean-ups and block parties, and grew a magnificent garden of corn, collard greens, and other vegetables in the yards behind Kelly Street. But we were getting nowhere with the local politicians. They scoffed at our plans. With the exception of one Council member, who was a socialist, they never admitted to the possibility that our plans were useful and could be successfully funded. No one took us seriously.

Bolder Action. Again, I went to U-HAB to vent my frustrations with Phillip St. Georges, whom I had forgiven for his earlier paycheck promise. Philip told me straight out that no one would ever take us seriously until we took bolder action. He stated that unless we physically took over the buildings we slated for renovation, our efforts would ultimately run out of steam.

This was difficult for me to accept. We had a great group of people. We were willing to back up our words with our muscles. Yet that wasn't good enough.

Now I was a self-proclaimed radical, but taking over publicly and privately-owned buildings seemed, at first, more than I was prepared to do. But the more we discussed it, the more it became clear that the group would soon disintegrate if we didn't take a dramatic step forward.

So in the summer of 1977, we "liberated" 936, 940 and 944 Kelly Street. It was a real thrill to break the seals of the buildings. Taking a sledgehammer to the concrete blocks was a dramatic step towards the redevelopment of the block. We had already arranged with Leon's father, Frank Potts, who owned six of the nine buildings on the east side of the block, to work in his buildings in exchange for containers he would get for us. Ultimately, he rented enough containers to allow us to clear out the garbage from 940 Kelly Street.

Luckily, some of President Johnson's War on Poverty programs had not yet been terminated. One such program, a Model Cities sanitation program, supplemented the regular sanitation service. Someone in our group knew workers from the Model Cities program, and we began a process that allowed us to clean out the garbage from most of the three buildings. One of the Model Cities Sanitation supervisors would come to our site and declare the alleyways and backyards a "rat hazard," allowing them to provide us with special disposal bags and to arrange for regular pick-ups once we filled all the bags they provided. Subsequently, we would discard more debris in the alleyways; the supervisor would visit and make the declaration anew, and we would get new bags, fill them up, and so on.

During that summer of 1977 we had lots of volunteers. Because of my connection to Casita Maria and the surrounding area, the group was fairly evenly mixed between black and Puerto Rican members. But over time, interest began to wane, leaving a core group of about thirty people, mostly black, and mostly from Kelly Street. Many were from the extended family of Frank Potts, who was the main reason why there was a block to organize around at all. He would often say proudly, "I have my blood in every one of these buildings."

Three people. Three people led the group: myself, Leon Potts, and Mildred Velez. Mildred was in her mid-twenties and willing to do volunteer work in return for getting an apartment. Leon was vested in the block because of his family and also because of his vision. He saw how we could create a community of people engaged in productive and mutually beneficial work.

He was also intrigued by the possibility of applying his plumbing and construction experience to areas of alternate energy and energy conservation, which were hot topics at the time – yes, thirty years ago! Many of the initial advocates for alternate energy came from local groups across the city and from similar inner city groups across the country. Many of these groups were engaged in self-help, sweat equity activities. Adopt-a-Building on the Lower East Side was in the process of installing the city's first tenement-roof windmill. They and PDC were also working on the installation of solar heating panels.

Besides being a full participant in the physical cleaning and gut demolition of the properties, I did most of the "outside work." This consisted of trying to obtain financial and political support for our efforts, bringing in technical help, and seeking out government assistance. I soon realized that the most outspoken of our members were also the shyest once they left the neighborhood. As a result, after countless plans to "all meet at the corner at 9 AM to travel to the meeting" (and I'd find that I was the only one there), I became resigned to being the public relations manager and official outside representative for our efforts.

We were among the most talented, creative, and dedicated groups I have ever encountered. But our efforts would have probably failed were it not for one event which we could not have possibly planned or predicted.

The President's Visit. On October 5, 1977, while a group of us were performing interior demolition at 940 Kelly Street, suddenly, helicopters flew overhead and a motorcade zoomed past our block. Later that day, we learned that President Jimmy Carter had toured the empty wasteland of Charlotte Street and had visited our friends at the Peoples Development Corporation across town in Morrisania. This event was the real beginning of our journey to becoming one of the most successful community development corporations in the country.

During the President's visit to Washington Avenue, he asked Ramon Rueda what he needed to build on his success at 1178 Washington Avenue, which by that time was inhabited and mostly completed. Ramon gave the obvious answer: they needed money.

Banana Kelly never directly benefited from the relatively generous federal response to that plea. But we indirectly benefited because after that, sweat equity became known as the "President's Program." I had previously submitted a grant application to the Citizens Committee for New York City, and shortly after the President's visit, we received what was at that time the largest Self Help Neighborhood Award Program grant to date – $900.

Just when I thought I would have to move in with my brother in Scarsdale, Banana Kelly received its first two contracts, one with the state and the other with the city. This allowed five or six of us to get paying positions in the newly incorporated Banana Kelly Community Improvement Association, Inc., and our work began in earnest.

We were able to move our office from the Settlement House to a first floor studio on Kelly Street. We purchased supplies and our first IBM Selectric typewriter. We established payroll, hired our first employees, and began recruiting youth between the ages of 16 and 19 for what was known then as the CETA Program.

The Comprehensive Employment and Training Act was a federal program designed to give employment and training to out-of-work adults. It was intended as a "counter-cyclical" program to provide training during periods of economic downturn. The particular program we were funded for under CETA was actually a youth program, and we were hiring young people to renovate houses.

We were in business.

Sweat Equity. We built on our success. In 1978 the city's housing budget included a "Sweat Equity" allocation, part of which was slated for our three buildings. We were approved for a new community management program called MIPP (Management in Partnership Program) that allowed us to take over property management services and eventually ownership of some of the buildings we organized in the neighborhood. We also had a weatherization program, a building "seal-up" program, a solar installation program, and more. In a very short period of time we were administering millions of dollars of public and private funds. I was twenty-five years old.

But progress, of course, was not steady, and that summer we narrowly averted disaster.

It was a hot day in July of 1978, and we had our youth workers busy in 940 Kelly Street. A number of us were in 944, making sure it was safe and preparing the site for the youth workers. We generally worked as a group or in pairs. That day, we were working in pairs, and Robert Foster and I were in a room on the 3rd floor of the building. All of a sudden, we heard what sounded like a gunshot. We immediately stopped working, looked around and noticed that the wall across from us was now sagging one inch below the ceiling. Robbie and I decided to empty the building, which we did. However, as we all stood outside on the sidewalk, I had second thoughts. I told Robbie that I thought that we should go back into the building so that if there was going to be an interior collapse we could somehow manage it and minimize the damage. He agreed.

We took two steps back into the building – and the entire interior of the building collapsed, from the fourth floor all the way down into the basement. Dust and debris – along with the two of us – came flying out of the building. The dust cloud spread to the surrounding blocks. To this day, if you look from Beck Street to the rear of 944 Kelly Street, you will see that the rear of that building is one storey lower than the adjoining buildings, a permanent memorial to an event which could have ended the program – to say nothing of our lives.

But we didn't entirely avoid tragedy.

Johnny and Dwayne. The CETA Program that we operated was designed to help young men and women. Mildred Velez gave up a good job as a legal secretary to become the director of the program. Most of our participants were seventeen and eighteen years old. When we recruited, we were inundated with applications, so we were able to be selective about whom we chose. All in all, we had a terrific group of people. The young men and women quickly became committed to the work we were doing, and one group even had a contest about arriving early to work. They were supposed to be there by eight-thirty. When they began showing up before seven, we put a stop to the contest.

At the end of each day, this group would always decide who got the most work done and who got the dirtiest. On both counts, Johnny Rodriguez usually won. Johnny stood out. He worked hard, laughed hard and was always good-natured.

But Johnny never got to finish the program.

Johnny and his family lived on Intervale Avenue, one block south of the elevated #2 line. Late one Friday night, while several of his extended family members were staying over, there was a fire in the kitchen. Flames quickly engulfed the three-storey, wood frame house. Johnny escaped the fire and stood on the overhang to the front porch of his building. Standing about ten feet from the ground he could have easily jumped to safety. But he shouted down to find out if his cousins had escaped, and he learned that some of them were still inside. Johnny re-entered the inferno.

The funeral was devastating. The viewing room was lined with eight caskets, and one of them held Johnny. To this day, I think of Johnny Rodriguez, that happy young man so full of life and potential. He had one foot in the new South Bronx and one foot in the old, and by his own choice, he perished for the love of his family.

I also think about Dwayne Jackson, another of our young stars. As far as I know, this young man had never picked up a tool before joining the program, but he had a seemingly inherent talent for plumbing. You didn't even need to show him how to do something; he already knew a better way. But I worried about Dwayne's personal life. He lived with the mother of his child. They were not married, but he was by all accounts devoted to her and gave her all his money. Apparently, she spent it mostly on herself and on her independent social life. Dwayne began showing up late for work. You could tell he was troubled. One day he discovered that she was having an affair and planned to leave him. He killed her then took his own life.

We mourned Johnny, and we mourned Dwayne. These were our tragedies. But most of our group thrived, and many of our trainees went on to make successful lives for themselves. Some became independent contractors, and others worked successfully in the construction trades. The CETA program had long-term benefits.

Encountering Helena. The Banana Kelly Community Improvement Association also had long term benefits to me on a personal level. While working at Banana Kelly, I came to know the woman who would become my wife.

Actually, my first encounter with Helena took place two years earlier. I was sitting aloof on a stoop on Kelly Street, and she and some others were engaged in a water fight. Suddenly, this cute young woman doused me with water – and went on her way while I was still shaking myself off.

Sometime later, I was giving a talk in the backyards of Kelly Street, urging those in attendance not to be chased from the neighborhood by the fires; to stand up and fight and take control of their destinies; to believe in this neighborhood's redevelopment; and to stay and become a part of that redevelopment. I told them: "Don't Move, Improve" – which became our group's slogan. Helena listened attentively.

We began to see one another. Soon, I fell in love with her and her three children, whom I have had the privilege to help raise. At the time, Christopher was nine years old. He is currently a captain in the Marines. Chantel was seven years old and is now an Emergency Medical Technician. KoySean was six years old and is presently the General Manager for Charlie Brown's steakhouse in Westchester. They are all married with children.

By 1981, Banana Kelly was well established, and I was looking for another challenge. By now, I had married Helena. I was twenty-eight years old, and I felt the time I had left for saving the world was dwindling. There were other reasons why I believed it was time for a change.

Success at a Price. Banana Kelly, almost overnight, had become very successful. But success came with a price. In the process of quickly going from an entirely volunteer effort to a funded organization, the dynamics of our group had changed substantially. By 1981, our volunteer base was small and mostly limited to event planning and participation on the board of directors of Banana Kelly and on the member-run, low-income corporation (a Housing Development Fund Company) that was now the owner of 936-940 and 944 Kelly Street. Banana Kelly had become an established community development corporation, or CDC.

In the process of this growth, our leaders became managers, our organizers became employees, and our members became clients. This disturbed me greatly because I believed then, as I do now, that any community organization is only as strong as the resources it has to back up its work. Those resources must consist of at least one of three elements:

1. strong, established institutional backing, such as a church;
2. financial resources;
3. membership.

We never had institutional backing or extensive financial resources, and we had lost our membership base through the unconscious and circumstantial processes leading to becoming a successful CDC. We were living off our competence and our utility. If we lost any substantial degree of competence, or if our work was no longer viewed by those in power as being important, we would lose our funding base. I believed it was necessary to revive the guarantor of our long term health and survival – namely our membership.[2]

However, I also believed that I, personally, could not make this happen, and, more importantly, that it would not happen for as long as I remained CEO. The transformation from volunteer/citizen group to CDC had created a substantial strain between me and the core leadership and membership. I was the one person at Banana Kelly capable of managing our contracts and contacts from the "outside." As I made commitments and took each commitment to heart, I used my position of Executive Director to force our group leaders, now our managers, to either perform or leave. Some stayed, others left. By 1981, what started in 1977 as cooperative and mutually supportive relationships became openly antagonistic. I believed there had to be a reconciliation between the staffed and funded organization and those that represented the initial membership and board of directors before we could revive and expand our membership base. So in June of 1981 I gave the Banana Kelly board a six-month notice of my intention to resign, effective January 1, 1982.

The Flawless Transition. I designed what I thought to be a flawless transition plan, with new staffing procedures and training for board members to solicit and interview candidates for a new Executive Director. At the end of this process, the best candidate would be the perfect Executive Director.

---

[2] A concern of many within community development who believed at that time that the long term viability of the field was dependent upon the active, engaged, and (when necessary) strident participation of residents. See, Robert Schur, *Back to Basics: Organizing in the Age of Austerity*, City Limits Magazine, January 1982, page A14.

The Concept of Community

But when it comes to human dynamics, all the planning and programming in the world cannot guarantee the right outcome. The training was so rigorous that some of the board members resigned once a new Executive Director was chosen. In addition, the person we chose was a good woman, but she had no experience in housing. I thought we had sufficient housing expertise within the organization to make up for her lacking and that instead of serving as the consummate housing professional, she would become an organizing force within Banana Kelly. She would help secure our long term viability. Once again, big mistake.

Almost immediately, the new Executive Director had problems with the staff, including Leon Potts, who was then the Director for our Weatherization Program and whose employment she ultimately terminated. She also had a standing feud with our construction supervisor. In January of 1982, I was brought onto the board of directors and heard stories about terrible arguments between them. I tried to intervene, but I was not successful. Then one day the fighting stopped, and she told me that their working relationship was now productive and cordial.

I was relieved. Then one afternoon I saw one of our own employee/maintenance workers coming out of a ground floor apartment of 1244 Westchester Avenue. I was still reviewing contracts and signing checks for Banana Kelly, so I remembered that the renovation of this particular apartment was being done by an outside contractor. I asked the worker what he and the others were doing in the apartment. He explained that they were doing all of the renovation.

I visited the office and asked to see the files. A new firm with which I had no familiarity was now our primary outside contractor, getting almost all the renovation work we contracted to outside companies. One such contract was for the renovation of 1244 Westchester Avenue.

After some investigation, it became obvious to me that either our Construction Supervisor had set up his own company or that he was working with one that already existed. By giving contracts to this firm and using Banana Kelly maintenance personnel to do the actual work, the firm only had to buy the materials – resulting in a profit margin of 40 to 60% on every job. I was pretty sure that the property manager, who had to sign off on the work, was also involved in this scam. To this day I do not believe that our Executive Director took part in or had any knowledge of what was going on – though as head of our entire operation, it was her responsibility.

So, eight months after the transition that resulted from "the perfect process," the board terminated three of our top managers, none of whom were part of the original Banana Kelly group, and called me back as Interim Director while we advertised for a new Executive Director.

The Ideal Candidate. This time, the board agreed that we absolutely needed a candidate who had housing experience. Getz Obstfeld, who had family ties to real estate in Brooklyn and had just completed a successful self-help renovation project in Rhode Island, seemed like the ideal candidate, and we hired him. Banana Kelly's membership was never revived, but the organization went on to grow from the $ 3 to 5 five million organization it was in 1982 to a $60+ million organization in 2001.

In 1985, I was accepted at New York Law School, and I resigned from the Board of Banana Kelly. A few months later, I heard that there was a move by a local power broker to take over the board of Banana Kelly. I worked in the background, primarily with the chair of the board, Elba Melendez, to stop this, since I believed that such a takeover would turn the organization from a community service organization into a patronage mill. By a very narrow vote, the effort was defeated and Banana Kelly's independence and reputation was preserved.

But as a result of this near takeover, Getz must have realized his political vulnerability and sought to strengthen the board to prevent this type of thing from happening again.

Sounds Perfect, Right?

At around this time, Yolanda Rivera came onto the board. She was a Connecticut government housing official who had grown up in the neighborhood, had family in the neighborhood, and had been a 7A Administrator for her own former building. This means she was a court-appointed receiver who collected rent and made repairs in buildings abandoned by their landlords.

Sounds perfect, right?

To this day I do not know if Getz found her or she found Getz. At any rate, soon Yolanda would rise to the dual role of Board Chairperson and CEO of Banana Kelly. Over the years, she would move authority for one program after another from Getz to herself. Getz was adept at developing housing projects and putting together funding packages for them. He put together a staff that would expand Banana Kelly's portfolio from less than 100 units in 1982 to about 1,000 units by the mid-nineties. But Yolanda continued to control the operations, eventually causing Getz's resignation and nearly destroying the organization in the process.

By the mid-nineties, Banana Kelly had received scores of millions of dollars in local, state and federal funds that Yolanda used to consolidate her own power and influence. She was ultimately removed by Eliot Spitzer, which is when I became involved in Banana Kelly again, the subject of a later chapter.

My early experience at Banana Kelly – the successes, the mistakes, and the power plays – would prove invaluable to my future work in the field.

III A Community Development Primer

To my knowledge, there is no definitive history of community development. The work that comes closest is *Corrective Capitalism*,[3] a report written for, and published by, the Ford Foundation. In that seminal report, the authors define community development as a countervailing balance to the excesses of free market capitalism. The organizations doing this work are referred to as "Community Development Corporations" or "CDCs." The authors explain that "in this free enterprise nation they [CDCs] are finding ways to open doors to classes of individuals otherwise excluded from the American Dream." Twenty years later, this sentiment still motivates the vast majority of CDCs. In the Forward of the report, Franklin A. Thomas, former President of the Ford Foundation (and, before that, President of the Bedford-Stuyvesant Restoration Corporation), defines CDCs through a set of characteristics:

> ... they operate within a geographically defined low income target area; they are controlled by the people who live in that area; and they undertake housing and economic development projects in addition to providing... social services...[4]

---

[3] Neal R Peirce and Carol F. Steinbach, *Corrective Capitalism, The Rise of America's Community Development Corporation,* The Ford Foundation, New York, 1987.
[4] *Ibid*, page 4.

If CDCs operate in low income areas and are controlled by people in those areas, it is logical to conclude that CDCs are, by definition, controlled by low income people. Today, unfortunately, resident control is the exception rather than the rule.

The Seventies. I started my work in community development in the mid seventies, at a time when the federal government had just instituted its second and final moratorium on mass-produced public housing development. The first, instituted sometime earlier by then-HUD Secretary George Romney, was technically necessary because rising inflation had pushed construction costs beyond the limits allowed by the authorizing legislation. However, it was no secret that the Nixon administration favored an end to what many conservatives considered a New Deal socialist experiment, and took full advantage of continued rising costs to kill the program once and for all. At about the same time, New York State, with the near collapse of its major housing development entity, the Urban Development Corporation, temporarily removed itself from the housing production business. And New York City was functionally bankrupt, coming under receivership by the state, and locked out of the capital bond markets. Obviously, community development efforts were severely challenged.

For help, I turned to a Model Cities group. The Model Cities program was part of President Johnson's War on Poverty, and it created the expectation that local groups engaged in anti-poverty programs would be directly funded by the federal government. Its credo was "maximum feasible participation" for program recipients, including the direct opportunity for them to run these programs.

At the time of Banana Kelly's inception, some Model Cities groups were still active in the South Bronx, and one of them had an office just around the corner from ours. The group was known as the Kelly Street Block Association, or KBA. We decided to share our plans with them for the sweat equity development of the vacant buildings on our street, so a group of us met with the director. She scoffed at our plans, which were embodied in a short position paper. I remember her saying, *"That* is not a plan." She then pointed to a long shelf of dust-laden binders containing urban renewal proposals and said, *"This* is a plan!" We left her office dejected. But KBA was living in the past, and it would not be long before Banana Kelly eclipsed this Model Cities group, which eventually went out of business.

The mid and late seventies were tumultuous years. Perhaps because it was a time of violently changing urban landscape and scant public funds, true community development flourished. Many new groups formed in a direct response to landlord abandonment, government retrenchment, resident flight, crime and arson. When conditions were truly terrible, many residents fled, but many others organized and fought back.

The Eighties. By the mid-eighties, the fiscal crisis in New York City was ebbing and there was increased pressure on the city to provide more housing for the poor. Local CDCs started pressing the city to do more, and many civic organizations and church groups clamored for aid, especially for the homeless, now a growing problem pressing on the public consciousness. Suddenly, the conventional idea of a homeless person changed from the Bowery bum to the woman on the street with two children and no place to call home.

It was at this time that a number of forces combined to both improve the prospects for further CDC growth and mark the beginning of the disconnect between community leaders and community. As an example, in the early eighties, the Banana Kelly Community Improvement Association was a $3 million organization with a staff of about 12 overseeing about 100 housing units with annual operating budgets of less than $1 million. After a decade of tapping into the opportunities provided by expanded city housing production and preservation programs, as well as the federal tax credit program, Banana Kelly grew to a $60 million organization with 100 employees overseeing 1,000 units of housing, with annual operating budgets in excess of $ 8 million. During this expansion, Banana Kelly went from a membership corporation with extensive resident participation to a full-service CDC, with residents participating in the organization merely as service recipients. This growth, in and of itself, might have been seen as an unqualified success. However, with this explosive growth came a shift in the relationship between Banana Kelly (as the local CDC) and the residents of the area. Banana Kelly began employing questionable social service theories, using "health realization" and "values clarification" techniques to help manage Banana Kelly's residents – treating them more like asset-deficient, service-dependent clients, than active stakeholders in their own institution.[5]

In New York City, an economic boom was beginning, with the city logging in budget surpluses for several years in a row. By 1986, the city was able to get back into the capital bond markets, which meant that it could once again begin to design and finance its own housing programs. At the time, I was part of a coalition of housing advocacy and development groups called the Housing Justice Campaign [HJC]. We put together a proposal calling on the city to make a major investment in the redevelopment and preservation of affordable housing units. We were given the opportunity to work with Mark Willis, Deputy Commissioner of the City's Department of Housing and Preservation and Development (HPD). We met with him throughout that summer. The Executive Director of Banana Kelly, Getz Obstfeld, and I were responsible for coordinating HJC's proposal based upon the needs expressed by our extensive membership and upon the outcomes of official discussions we were having with the city.

As mentioned above, there were many groups pressuring the city to get more involved in affordable housing preservation and production. But there were also groups pushing for middle income housing. Many of these advocates were from inner city areas such as the South Bronx whose consistent claim was "we've got enough low income housing in our area!" HJC was probably the most comprehensive of the advocacy groups, since it was inclusive of CDCs, church groups, homeless advocates, and social service organizations. The overriding call of the group was that city funds should be targeted based upon need and that the city funds should be used for a mix of incomes representing all

---

[5] Health Realization is a concept developed by Roger C. Mills and George Pransky in the 1980s that focuses on inner thought and how it can define and actualize life experiences. Values Clarification is a concept developed in the 1960s, but mostly applied in mental health and educational settings. Application of the concept has been criticized for varied and inconsistent reasons, ranging from forcing values on people to promoting acceptance of moral relativism.

those most in need of housing assistance as well as those most at risk of homelessness. Most of all, the group believed no city funds should be used for housing those who were capable of housing themselves

Tables Turned. In the early Fall of 1986, after months of meetings, we met with Mark Willis and were told that the city was ready to make its announcement of a 10-year, $4.2 billion housing plan that would target two populations – the homeless and the middle class. We were overwhelmed by the size of the plan (it was unprecedented in scope) and distraught because all the work we had done with HPD throughout the summer was dismissed. We were appalled that the needs of poorly-housed low-income people were being ignored. We felt that the City's plan had many problems: concentrating the homeless in targeted neighborhoods, ignoring the large segment of the population most at risk of becoming homeless, and using public monies for the middle class, which could still house itself.

We called an impromptu press conference and revealed the city's plan. HPD officials felt that we had betrayed their confidence by announcing the plan before the Mayor could do so. They quickly added a third program to help those of low and moderate income to their plan. The city would never admit to this and held firm to the position that these three programs were their intention all along, but the third program was added in direct response to our criticism and action.

After the Mayor's press event, some of the Housing Justice Campaign leaders were punished. At this time, I was working for the Parodneck Foundation, so I was punished by having the Parodneck Foundation's already approved contract with the city delayed for several months. We were serving senior citizen homeowners in need of critical repairs. It took the intervention of Ron Shiffman to free up the contract that Paul Crotty, the HPD Commissioner at the time, had refused to sign. Over the next few months, the contract just sat on his desk while the Parodneck Foundation absorbed the cost of the program's operation.

But in spite of this rocky start, the city's re-entry into the housing production and preservation market proved a real boon for neighborhoods and for the city's CDCs, many of which experienced the kind of ten-fold growth experienced by Banana Kelly during the same period

The Federal Housing Tax Credit Program. While the city was undertaking its newly ambitious foray into the production and preservation of housing, a new housing tax credit program was instituted at the federal level that would revolutionize the manner in which low income housing was developed. The Federal Housing Tax Credit Program was and is a tax incentive program, allowing qualified investors (mostly corporations) to take passive ownership of qualified low income housing development projects. In return for investing what usually amounts to a mere third of the total development cost of a project, they received all of the deductions active housing investors received, with much less risk involved, along with tax credits over a 10-15 year period. Suffice it to say that this program was very well-received by investors, all of whom were large corporations. One bank official at Republic National Bank (now HSBC), informed me that selling these kinds of deals to her community investment committees were "no-brainers" since the investing corporation realized $3 to $4 for every $1 invested over the term of the tax credit period.

The explosive growth in the availability of federal low income tax credits, which soon became the dominant means of developing low income housing, led to some two million low income units produced nationally in the next twenty years.

CDC Growth Leads to New Challenges. The city's new housing programs, low income tax credits and other opportunities forced CDCs to either fall by the wayside or to take advantage of these new opportunities for housing development. But this choice came at a price that goes to the core of what a community development corporation is and who it serves.

In 1989, Ron Shiffman, at the time the Director of the Pratt Center in Brooklyn, wrote a paper for a conference held at the New School for Social Research (now the New School University) in New York City. Ron agreed with Peirce and Steinbach, as well as with other authors on the subject, in plac-

The Concept of Community

ing the birth of the so-called "CDC Movement" with the emergence of such groups as the Bedford-Stuyvesant Restoration Corporation in the late sixties. He saw the emergence of CDCs as a "key outcome of these Great Society programs." He went on to define CDCs more broadly than Pearce and Steinbach, essentially seeing them as integrative and comprehensive vehicles for dealing with all of a neighborhood's needs – "social, economic, and physical."[6]

Ron has been a good friend for almost 30 years. We have been involved in many community struggles together, and I have the utmost respect for him. However, I think that his analysis and conclusions lend themselves to the view that it is the job of society, its leaders, and its government to provide a framework and atmosphere to permit community development to exist and flourish. He states:

> Strong local institutions provide the framework for the necessary social organization to take place and provide for the avenues of opportunity necessary for residents of low-income communities to develop.[7]

While this is consonant with some progressive theories, I believe Shiffman has it backwards. He states that strong local institutions create "social organization" (i.e. community). This position is inconsistent with history and also contrary to the mechanisms of true community development. Institutions are a means to accomplish the community's enunciated agenda. If there is no community to begin with, you cannot create one by first developing local institutions. If you attempt to build the institution before you build community, the institution will most likely exclude community in any real sense.

I am sometimes asked, "How can community exist without institutions?" In a community, lives are intertwined and interconnected. When there is a need, individuals can contribute time, labor, goods, tools, whatever and collectively

---

[6] Ronald Shiffman, "Comprehensive and Integrative Planning for Community Development, A Discussion Paper for the Community Economic Development Study Conference Research Center," New School for Social Research, June 14, 1989 (www.picced.org/advocacy/compplan.htm).
[7] *Ibid*, p. 6.

accomplish a desired result – without any institutions having been established. It is only when collective needs (such as education and security) become ongoing that a community starts establishing institutions to operate more efficiently. These institutions are supported through systems of voluntary assessments – or through taxes.

Developing Local Leaders. "Leadership Development" is a favorite funding target among philanthropies that fund community development work. The tendency to fund leadership development, similar to providing outside support for institutional development, is based upon a belief that community exists and merely lacks the tools necessary to maximize the potential for local enhancement.

As with developing institutions in the absence of community, looking to develop leaders in its absence will preclude true community leadership from ever occurring. Leadership evolves and is sustained through the structure and processes of community. To develop leadership first tends to "fix" leadership and embody it semi-permanently in chosen individuals.

In a true community setting, there is no need to assign or develop a leader or leadership group. Within a functioning community, different leaders emerge at different times, given their circumstances, talents and experience. Once a given challenge is met, the leaders retreat to being members of the community once again.

By developing the leadership and building an institution, such as local employment and career-enhancement center, prior to building community, the institution may provide some form of service and a semblance of community to local residents, but the sustaining basis of that service will have to be provided from the outside through grants, contracts, and other forms of fee-based income. This is because the institution is barren from within – there is no community. And the absence of community is concomitant with the local residents' loss of political power, which is why philanthropic support is so readily appreciated and sought after.

Two Books on CDCs. In their book, *Comeback Cities*,[8] Paul Grogan and Tony Proscio provide a more recent and comprehensive look at CDCs. They make the case that community development as we know it today began with the community groups that arose through implementation of the "War on Poverty" programs in the sixties and early seventies. Again, this perspective is consonant with that of Shiffman and Peirce/Steinbach. But Grogan and Proscio also posit that these early groups were often run by "exploitative imitators"[9] and "racial demagogues"[10] who were mostly taken up with demanding control over public resources and decision-making. They claim that these groups were organized primarily to

> oppose private investment, and seeking to preserve local concentrations of poverty (in the name of maintaining affordability) rather than developing integrated communities where profit and subsidies could coexist.[11]

The authors go on to explain that these efforts and their leaders (for the most part) failed, and that they were replaced by more rational, inclusive and forward-thinking grass roots leaders who developed practices that focus on cooperation instead of confrontation.

In an earlier work, Robert Halpern[12] holds a similar theory, but he has a more generous explanation for the sixties goal of preserving low income areas. By his reasoning, this new form of organization came about as a result of a return to "nineteenth century utopian and communitarian thought and... the efforts of early twentieth century black leaders"[13] who eschewed integration in favor of bolstering the wealth and independence of local black communities.

As did Grogan and Proscio, Halpern sees the modern-day CDCs as evolving from the protest efforts of the sixties and early seventies, but the more

---

[8] Paul S. Grogan and Tony Proscio, *Comeback Cities*, Westview Press, 2000.
[9] *Ibid*, p. 60.
[10] *Ibid*, p. 66.
[11] *Ibid*, p. 70.
[12] Robert Halpern, *Rebuilding the Inner City*, Columbia University Press, 1995.
[13] *Ibid*, p.128.

modern CDCs were more mature, more accommodating, and more apt to seek integration into the mainstream economy (through niche economic development emphases). And they

> opted for a more cooperative, 'businesslike' approach in their projects, appealing to the self-interest and latent social conscience of established institutions.[14]

Nonetheless, to state, as Halpern does, that these organizations grew up "out of their own efforts to define their own needs, control their own fate, and create viable local communities,"[15] seems a bit of a stretch, especially when he considers the Bedford-Stuyvesant Restoration Corporation to be exhibit A. From 1968 through 1974 Bed-Stuy received tens of millions of dollars from the federal government alone for its comprehensive array of programs. Since 1974, the Ford Foundation and other private and public sources have advanced additional tens of millions of dollars in grants and program related investments to Bed-Stuy. In many ways, Bed-Stuy and other similar so-called "first generation CDCs" seem to have approached community economic development in much the same that Community Action Agencies ultimately approached health and social services, which is to say that this seems to contrast greatly with a contention of such early CDCs developing out of "their own efforts." Or at least this would appear to be the case from the available record.

I had the opportunity to discuss this at some length with Ron Shiffman, who as a 25 year old graduate student, was intimately involved in the early development of Bedford-Stuyvesant. Ron stated to me that the documented history of what most consider to be the first CDC (the Bedford Stuyvesant Restoration Corporation), is actually a revisionist history, written to promote Robert Kennedy's need for a more top-down and less strident leadership at the local level. In fact, Ron's story is one that is consistent with similar local efforts – efforts that are built upon integrated and coordinated efforts led mostly by local women, until funding comes available, at which time the "matriarchy" is sup-

---

[14] *Ibid*, p. 139.
[15] *Ibid*, p. 126.

planted and replaced by more "responsible leadership." But much was accomplished, in spite of the undercutting of the local leadership. Among many other things, a single Congressional District was created to better represent the interests of Central Brooklyn, which became the platform for Shirley Chisholm's groundbreaking political career. If not for the efforts of the local leadership, New York City would likely have received Model Cities designation for only one area – Harlem. Finally, the grass roots efforts pushed for a local institutional model to implement what was soon to become Model Cities – thus providing for the precedent for a Community Development Corporation model of community development.

Halpern goes on to speak of the evolution of the CDC movement.

In their own continuing development efforts CDCs found that the most promising strategy was to stay small and to seek out specialized market niches.[16]

I have been doing this work for over 30 years, and I never met anyone who purposefully kept their operations "small" as a strategic approach to community development. As with Grogan and Proscio, Halpern credits the Ford Foundation as having a major role, allowing the development of CDCs to be coordinated from above. This was simply not the case in New York City. From the 1970s onward, CDCs besides the Bedford-Stuy and the Local Initiative Support Corporation (LISC) were hard-pressed to even get an audience with the Ford Foundation.

Pandering for Philanthropy. Most community development efforts that I am familiar with grew out of a perceived crisis and the recognition that conventional means would not lead to positive change. Also, beyond the initial federal funding of CDCs in the late sixties and early seventies, most CDCs functioned in an (initial) environment of government austerity (or in the case of New York

---

[16] *Ibid*, p.139.

City, near-bankruptcy), economic recession, bank closings, business relocation, landlord abandonment and public policy atrophy. That is the real reason why so many CDCs remained small for so long – they were responding to the absence of the public and private sectors in their neighborhoods as opposed to responding to a re-channeling of existing resources through their organizations.

I view the emergence of community development differently from the authors I have discussed. I disagree that the field of community development began in the Model Cities era and evolved into community development as we know it today. Instead, I see these as two distinct development patterns, with the earlier CDCs that survived having adapted to the circumstances under which the current crop of CDCs developed in the first place. And I certainly disagree with the notion that current community development efforts were basically built on cooperation with government, banks, and business interests.

I am reminded of a lecture I attended where Michael Eichler, currently the Director of the Consensus Organizing Center and professor at San Diego State University, promoted the benefits of "consensus organizing" as opposed to "confrontational organizing." His point was exactly the same as that made by Grogan and Proscio – that confrontation is counter-productive, builds walls between parties that need to cooperate, and becomes a self-defeating end.

The experience he cited to make his point was one with which I had some familiarity, and I asked him if he thought that his "consensus" organizing drive would have been as successful if the Association for Community Organizations for Reform Now (ACORN), a national organizing group, was not in the same area, organizing around the same issues, but in a confrontational manner. He then agreed, speculating that in the absence of ACORN's aggressive, confrontational tactics, his organizing might not have succeeded.

More radical groups often help mainstream groups achieve their ends. In New York City, the Gay Men's Health Crisis, a mainstream, "rational," consensus-building group, would have been much less effective without the existence of ACT-UP – a direct action, take-no-prisoners, in-your-face, confrontational organization.

The Concept of Community

I remember my own experience with ACORN in New York City. Fresh from a successful squatter campaign in Philadelphia, ACORN initiated one in the East New York section of Brooklyn. A deputy commissioner from the city's housing department, Joel Shuldiner, invited me to negotiate a new program that would have directly undercut ACORN's organizing effort. The city offered my group an initial $1 million contract and complete control over direction of those funds and the program, and I suppose I could have agreed. If I had, I could have subsequently gone on to sing the praises of my mature "consensus-building" approach over ACORN's irrational and immature "confrontational approach." I could have pointed to the success of a funded program and renovated homes as proof of the superiority of my more rational and productive approach.

Instead, I left that meeting telling Shuldiner that I would seriously consider the offer and that he could feel free to represent that we were in discussions. A few days later, Mayor Koch, announced that my organization was being awarded $1 million to administer a "low income auction program" in the East New York section of Brooklyn. It was then that I woke up to the city's actual intention of cutting out ACORN entirely. My response was to provide the city with a housing proposal that included ACORN as a partner in the redevelopment effort. As a result, over 300 units of housing were developed in what is still the single largest and most successful scattered-site homesteading program in New York City. Throughout the Koch administration we were unable to use ACORN's name in any public releases or official documents. But in spite of their official anonymity, ACORN was able to operate the program and serve its members. Since that time, they have gone on to develop other housing programs in New York City without having to work in the background. They have also played a major role in the formation of a new political party, the Working Families Party, and many politicians actively sought their endorsement. In fifteen years, New York ACORN went from a group of squatters whom politicians scorned and ignored to a major housing developer and political kingmaker.

There are times to cooperate and times to confront. Neither tactic can be eschewed in favor of the other.

Consensus-building as an organizing approach resonates well with foundation officials who are by nature conservative and adverse to the risks inherent in confrontational organizing. Consultants and groups that promote consensus-organizing do well with funders who, for the most part, want to promote change but see change as occurring for dysfunctional people and dysfunctional areas. Many foundation board members are good people, but they see it as their duty to help people fix their problems, most often starting with fixing the people themselves. Confrontational organizing suggests that the problem exists outside, as opposed to inside, the community.

Beyond Alinsky. When I was an organizer for the Northwest Bronx Community and Clergy Coalition in the early seventies, those of us learning how to effectively organize spent a considerable amount of time studying and practicing the tactics of the great community and labor leader Saul Alinsky. His style of organizing was confrontational, operating on the assumption that there is potential redress of any problem by directing a campaign towards the source (or closely related to the source) of the wrong that a group seeks to right. However, when I moved from the Northwest Bronx to the Southeast Bronx, I quickly found that these tactics were useless in an environment where there was no one to mobilize against. It was as if he had developed the best recipe for stew in the wilderness – and the ingredients simply weren't available. There was nothing wrong with the recipe, but it was irrelevant to the South Bronx.

Who were we supposed to fight against? The city was nearly bankrupt and losing control of its own budgeting and financing powers. Landlords were abandoning their properties by the thousands. The courts were of little use when "paper ownership" in buildings changed constantly. There were no banks with mortgages to protest against. In short, there was no redress possible from any third party. The only alternatives were to flee or to take on the problem ourselves, and to me, this recognition marks the true beginning of the community development movement in the South Bronx and similar inner city areas.

Should Banana Kelly fight against some faceless landlord, dysfunctional government agency or uncaring bank or insurance company? This seemed pointless. Instead, we decided to save, rebuild, and sustain our community on our own.

Doing It Ourselves. So instead of organizing rent strikes against the landlord, we collected voluntary payments from residents to pay utility bills, supply heat, and sweep and mop hallways. We pooled small amounts of money to obtain deeds to buildings that would be owned by residents and CDCs. We urged people to stop hoping for public housing when the waiting list was more than ten thousand – and instead reclaim vacant buildings and turn them around. Instead of going to Housing Court, we took community control of buildings in what Professor Robert Kolodny of Columbia University referred to as "ad hoc tenant" management.[17] We stopped complaining about no heat and instead installed solar panels and windmills. We didn't picket the local substandard supermarket for better produce and lower prices ; we created community gardens, food cooperatives and investigated Community Supported Agriculture (CSA). CSA was a program where groups provide money to a farmer before the growing season in return for fresh produce at a much-reduced cost when the crops are harvested. (It was a good idea, but in actuality, it didn't work well in our neighborhood.)

If the government, the courts, the landlords, and elected officials were helpless to redress local concerns, then the residents themselves would have to solve their own problems. This change in approach from organizing for redress from some third party to self-help is much more than a change from confrontational to consensus organizing. At Banana Kelly, we took control of buildings from landlords before they had the opportunity to torch or take needed resources (cash flow, copper pipes, insurance proceeds) from their buildings. Other groups did the same. I remember heated calls from owners threatening me with bodily harm and accusing me and my colleagues of being communists. Nor did we "build consensus" with the local drug dealers. They were told to

---

[17] See *Self Help in the Inner City: A Study of Lower Income Cooperative Housing Conversion in New York,* United Neighborhood Houses of New York, Inc. 1973.

leave the premises or risk getting thrown off the roof, an option that was often threatened but never exercised.

In the mid seventies, Banana Kelly's motto became "Don't Move, Improve!" I have seen this motto used in Northwest Bronx and other parts of the country as well. The motto signaled new brand of community development. It emerged from the common motivation of community organizers around the country.

In New York City, many neighborhoods seemed destined for oblivion. But they survived and provided the local leadership for resurgence. If you visit the "lower 900 block" of Kelly Street today, it seems overly dense given the immediately surrounding neighborhood. But that block is representative of the density of the Hunts Point-Longwood neighborhood before fires ravaged the area. An extraordinary effort on the part of the Banana Kelly residents led to the extraordinary survival of a block.

But that does not explain the revival of the neighborhood as a whole – even considering the efforts of SEBCO, Mid-Bronx Desperados, Longwood Historic District Association, and the South Bronx Community Housing Corporation in the immediate area. Something else was also happening in scattered buildings throughout the South Bronx and other inner city areas of the city.

The Myth of Home Ownership. When I was still Executive Director of Banana Kelly, I personally escorted housing commissioners, local and foreign students, journalists, planners, and reporters (as well as Governor Hugh Carey and David Rockefeller) on tours through the Hunts Point-Longwood neighborhood. During these tours, policy makers would sometimes marvel at the spattering of small homes that had survived within areas of terrible devastation. They would conclude that the reason these homes had survived was that they were small, owned by individuals, and occupied exclusively by family members. But I showed them that for every single-family or two-family house that survived, there were scores of units in multiple dwellings that were occupied and thriving. They survived because people in those buildings began collecting their own rents, paying their own fuel bills, securing their own entranceways, and generally protecting their homes. Survival within a devastated neighborhood is *not* a function of single-family home ownership but of control by the residents!

Nonetheless, on each tour I found myself arguing against the prevailing perception that the Bronx burned because it lacked home ownership. By home ownership, these visitors were referring to the kind of home ownership that prevails in suburbs. Cities such as New York City were viewed as anachronisms, and many believed that the only way for cities to survive was to re-create suburbia in the inner city.[18] This kind of thinking led to the creation of the New York City Housing Partnership by David Rockefeller and the Nehemiah Program by I.D. Robbins. These programs aimed to increase home ownership by using a combination of government grants of unused urban renewal land and forgivable government loans. These programs were not necessarily bad, but they were not the answer to redeveloping areas such as the South Bronx.

Low-Income Cooperatives and HDFCs. In the seventies and eighties, there were many individuals who took over landlord-abandoned buildings, most of which eventually became low-income cooperatives. Resident leaders such as Mildred Strickland, Ozenith Tate, Marie Thompson, Mary Blassingame and hundreds of others reclaimed and renovated buildings in the Bronx, Harlem, East Harlem and the Lower East Side. In many areas, these buildings and their leaders provided the glue that sustained a semblance of neighborhood. In most cases where an individual led a building from landlord abandonment to tenant ownership, that leader was a woman.

Many buildings taken by New York City for tax arrears had active tenant associations. For these (and others that subsequently got themselves organ-

---

[18] Oddly enough, today there is a trend in the opposite direction, and developers seem to have recognized the value of well-functioning city neighborhoods. According to a lead article in the *New York Times*, February 21, 2002, "lifestyle villages" are beginning to pop up throughout the country. These entities built by commercial developers offer studios, lofts, townhouses and villas. They are designed for two population segments – young, affluent professionals and retiring baby-boomers. There are no planned day care centers, schools, or playgrounds that would encourage residents to see these "communities" as places to raise children. These are fabricated "urban neighborhoods" that are mono-cultural, affluent, and unencumbered by school tax levies.

ized), a program for tenant ownership was created: these buildings were sold to tenant-controlled Housing Development Fund Corporations (HDFCs). Today, there are over 20,000 units that are owned by HDFCs, the majority controlled by residents.

Nationwide, many individuals chose to stay and fight for the survival and enhancement of their neighborhoods. Often the leaders were from local institutions, such as churches, with a fixed stake in the community and a claim to the "moral high ground." But people need a "spark" to work for change. And this spark – often generated by leadership – may come from within or without. In many instances – mine included, since I grew up on Long Island and moved into the neighborhood – the spark came from without the neighborhood. When it does come from within, the newly emerging leader has often had been exposed to life outside the area. He or she then returns and works to turn things around. In many cases, an outside perspective is necessary to induce change.

"Learned Helplessness." This is due to a basic human trait that is at once our greatest survival asset and our greatest impediment to change: our ability to adapt to our surroundings. This ability to adapt dulls our senses and removes our will to work for change. In environmental psychology this is called "learned helplessness." We accept our conditions, expect these conditions to remain, and learn to work through them. This is how we survive.

Learned helplessness explains why the protagonists of change are often outside organizers or local residents who served in the military or went away to school or jail and then returned home. In 1974 while I was studying with him, Reverend Paul Brandt of Fordham University maintained that it is *always* an outsider who brings change to a community. Nonetheless, I have seen cases where longtime residents were shocked out of their apathy by some dramatic event (the gunshot that almost hit a son, the fire that nearly claimed a life). These individuals then took action.

CDCs Today. Today, there is a remarkable infrastructure of CDCs throughout New York City and the nation. In the last ten to fifteen years, they have continued to provide quality housing as well as expanding into other areas such as job training, economic development, literacy training, social service, and legal help. Under the rubric of "comprehensive community initiatives," these groups have taken a holistic approach to community development. This is very promising.

It is equally promising that many young people are once again drawn to community development. My generation came into the job market in the early to mid-seventies, when many young people arose from and flocked to inner city neighborhoods and worked for radical change. From the mid-eighties through the nineties, however, young people were not drawn to this work. Today it is heartening to see young people once again at meetings with government and community agencies. It is also gratifying to hear young people speak with a world view that goes well beyond materialism and self-gratification.

On the downside, however, since the Reagan years, when some CDCs adopted a "bottom line approach," many have become overly-professionalized, with property management, case-management, and other services generating fees and the people in the neighborhoods becoming merely instruments of institutional enhancement.

What often happens is that the CDCs grow apart from the residents and operate without regard to the local community. As that occurs, the leadership becomes more distant from the constituency, future plans for work are externally-motivated and institutionally directed, and all programs and work efforts are dependent upon outside resources. Once this happens, the institution has made the complete transition from a community institution to an externally-directed, locally-based service institution.

In January, 2002, within two days I heard very similar stories told by two serious, intelligent and articulate young women from different community housing groups in New York City. The Bronx woman spoke of the problem of developing affordable housing, given the constraints of the various funding sources. It was just not possible to combine available public and private funding to get housing that was affordable to low income families and households. The Brooklyn woman also spoke of the difficulty in making some of her agency's programs work, given the low income restrictions of some of the funding sources.

"Low-income" is defined as households earning 80% of the area median income. In 2001, the median income in the New York metropolitan area for a family of four was nearly $60,000. Low income was thus defined as a household earning under $47,000 per year. In that year, the New York City median income was about $33,000 per year, making "low income" for over 3 million New Yorkers just over $26,000 per year.

Since "low income" households could not afford "low income" housing, both of these women proposed... *not* more government subsidies to make the programs work for the economically disadvantaged. No, each suggested that the "low income" restriction on the State and federal funding be raised from 80% to 100% of median income. The representatives were unapologetic in their proposed solution. The complexity of community development had been seen as a simple mathematical problem to be solved by a change in one variable, irrespective of the human consequences for residents relying on this local institution to serve their needs.

If a CDC is no more than a not-for-profit housing developer, and if development of "low income" housing is no more than the manipulation of numbers, then why do we need not-for-profit housing developers at all? The private, for-profit sector is well equipped to develop housing if provided with an appropriate level of public subsidies.

A few years ago I wrote an Op-Ed piece for *City Limits*, a New York magazine.[19] My point was that CDCs have transformed from community groups "that once focused on the demands of neighborhood residents" but now were primarily dedicated "to their own institutional growth." I went on to say:

> The sad fact is that currently most community housing groups no longer work for, represent, or even hold themselves accountable to the communities in which they work. There is very little work going into changing anything. We have all become managers of the crisis. In effect, this means that we merely compete against one

---

[19] DeRienzo, "Managing the Crisis," *City Limits Magazine*, December, 1994, p. 25.

another to manage different parts and amounts of the same problem. We succeed, not by the social change we promote and achieve, but by the size of our budgets, the programmatic reach of our institutions, and the scope of our activity. In the process of going from relevant and dynamic agents of change to proficient managers of the status quo, we have abandoned our missions and our communities.

The article went on to urge groups to reconnect with the residents they were created to serve. The further detached they were from their constituent base, the more vulnerable such groups were to the whims of outside funding entities. I have made the same point again and again over the years. In the long run, the health of a CDC is dependent on a few factors. If the CDC is institutionally connected (such as connected to a religious group or coalition of religious groups), then its survival is better ensured as long as the affiliated or sponsoring institution remains strong and sees continued value in the mission of the subsidiary institution. But if the CDC lacks an institutional sponsor, political sponsor, or financial patron, then it must have a strong constituent base in order to survive.

The CDC movement has its roots in the civil rights era. The movement itself grew during the seventies and eighties, times of fiscal austerity and government retrenchment. In the nineties, the CDCs came of age and flourished as developers of low income housing, primarily through the low income housing tax credit.

The challenge at the beginning of the 21st Century is for the CDCs to perform at a professional level while at the same time re-connecting to a constituent base and making themselves accountable to that base. The infrastructure is there and, for many, the motivation is there. But for CDCs to regain their legitimacy they must work to build community – the very thing their characterization as a particular kind of organization takes for granted. In the process of rebuilding community, they must transform their own character from local poverty managers to agents of change for the community they serve.

III Working Concepts and Definitions

Having worked in community development for thirty years, I have come to believe it is paramount to have a philosophical basis for this work. Without such a basis, it is too easy to fall into traps, such as turning a community effort into a mechanism for individual and institutional aggrandizement.

Taking "community" as a given – as is often done in pursuit of some "community" effort – is the equivalent of engaging in economic development and taking the economy for granted, or undertaking natural development and taking nature or the sciences for granted. Yet finding the right definition can be confounding.

The Two Extremes. On the one hand, there are philosophers who seem to define familiar concepts as intellectual riddles:

> In saying that community is the position of existence, we are saying that community is the position of the position. Indeed it is. We are saying that community is the decisive mode of positioning or position (and consequently, of being).[20]

Well, that certainly clarifies things.

---

[20] Jean-Luc Nancy, "Of Being-in-Common," p. 2, *Community At Loose Ends,* edited by the Miami Theory Collective, University of Minnesota Press, 1991.

On the other hand there are established and respected community developers who bandy about terms and concepts as though they were self-evident. It is not unusual to hear an executive say something like,

> Community is what we are doing when we bring our residents together and community-building represents the techniques we use to bring people together to attain common goals."

"Whatever I Want It to Be". The most cynical use of terminology I ever heard came from a priest (of all people!) working in the Highbridge section of the Bronx. He was planning a mutual housing development for the Archdiocese of New York, which was in the process of developing affordable rental housing near Yankee Stadium. Mutual housing means mutual control and/or ownership by the residents. The Archdiocese was working with a local group of residents organized by South Bronx People for Change, and the organizer for this group, Blanca Ramirez, brought me in as an advisor. At the time, there was frustration on both sides of the development, and it was clear that the Archdiocese was developing "mutual housing" only because it was popular with sponsors. I felt that the very basis of mutual housing (mutual control and/or ownership by the residents) was not being respected.

At one point, I had a discussion with the Archdiocese official in charge of the development. Finally, when he tired of my challenging him on the mutual housing issue, he flat out told me, "Mutual housing is whatever I want it to be!" For him, the ability to control the process and outcome within a programmatic framework made "mutual housing" his preferred approach to housing development, never mind its philosophical basis.

There has to be some middle ground, some critical analysis by which to guide and judge our work without getting lost in some metaphysical maze, on the one hand, or being trapped in circular reasoning and self-serving tautologies on the other.

Definitions as a Measure of Ideals. Over the years I have found it useful to develop working definitions and concepts to help me judge whether my practice is holding up to my ideals.

Take "community organizing." Am I organizing for some short term victory or, and preferably, am I organizing in order to develop a new set of arrangements that in the long term allow for collective power? Any organizer can mobilize people in the short run. The problem with short term organizing is that it raises expectations without any long-term benefit. Most such organizing efforts survive in one of only two ways: by the constant duplication of mobilizing efforts against new "enemies" or new causes or by sealing a victory with a funded program that often turns the agitating protestors into serviceable clients.

Open-Ended Organizing. Another question that I ask myself is whether a given organizational effort is open enough. Does the group truly decide its agenda? Collective deliberation allows for a sharing of problems and perspectives. Once this is done, individuals discover that they are not alone in how they feel. For those in oppressive circumstances, it is easy to believe that every problem is personal and, as such, nearly impossible to overcome. Collective discussions undertaken in safe public spaces strip away the mystery that often accompanies oppression. The feeling that "they" are doing this to oneself or that "they" would never allow one to succeed is replaced by a sense that there is an identifiable reason, source or motivation behind one's problems. Once the problem has a name, it can be addressed directly, confronted and possibly resolved. Talking with each other and identifying their common problems often leads people to take some form of action. This action has not been determined in advance.

Of course there are risks to such open-ended organizing. The dynamic can run totally out of control, regardless of how carefully the organizers have planned their work.

Exasperation with the threefold frustration of action – the unpredictability of its outcome, the irreversibility of the process, and the anonymity of its authors – is almost as old as recorded history.[21]

Many community leaders get around the "open-ended" problem by creating the façade of democratic participation while keeping the substance of decision-making to themselves. Within such circumstances, "action" is organized into discrete, limited and manageable components. Some groups organize around one ideal, or one approach or one agenda, and fight any deviation from the norm. Groups that focus on organizing and advocacy often find themselves in ethical dilemmas because of this. They purport to be progressive, grass roots organizations but they often end up superimposing the agenda, circumscribing the debate, and managing the outcomes. For many such groups, the fear that popular action will spiral out of control and result in unintended, unanticipated, and uncontrollable political consequences is joined by the fear that popular action will remove control from the advocates of those very same actions. So most groups organize around prescribed issues and agendas, using prescribed tactics, and seeking prescribed outcomes. But to prescribe is ultimately to manipulate and, to paraphrase Rousseau, to manipulate is to enslave.

Health-Realization and Values-Clarification. I am reminded of prevailing practice among some CDCs in the 1980s and 1990s of inventing or super-imposing a social-scientific basis for approaches to community development. They used the terms Health-Realization and Values-Clarification.

Health Realization is based upon solid reasoning: no group change can occur without certain changes occurring within the individuals of that group. However, the way in which the theory was used in practice was to maintain each resident as an isolated individual dealing with personal problems to be dealt with in a case-management manner. This was deemed a necessary precedent to broader community participation and collective action. This focus on the individual was debilitating to any true community development. To me,

---

[21] Hannah Arendt, *The Human Condition,* University of Chicago Press, 1958, 1998, p.220.

health realization and other such theories, while sounding good in proposals, are often little more than pseudo-science and in actuality amount to just another means to manage the poor.

Similarly, "Values Clarification" was used by Banana Kelly and other groups throughout much of the nineties. To become a tenant in a Banana Kelly building, tenants had to agree to a lease rider that framed individual shortcomings and bound the tenant, contractually, to overcome those shortcomings. For instance, in order to enter into a lease, a family would have to subscribe to a set of values that would be framed in the form of a contract. The contract would suggest itself as a binding agreement between Banana Kelly and the client, whereby the client would agree to address and resolve noted deficiencies regarding the client family's background. It was, of course, presumed that these personal deficiencies were the cause of the family's homelessness. So the adult family members entering into a lease would agree to make improvements in their personal lives (education, career advancement, involvement with their children's schools). The agreement also required that the adults attend "values clarifications classes," which were designed to create a hostile environment for any family suspected of harboring, supporting, or not reporting drug dealers.

Put together, "health realization" and "values clarification" were mostly used as means for the manipulation of residents and the personal benefit of the CDC leadership.

Visioning and Facilitators. For every "comprehensive community initiative," participatory planning is a key component. But at all of the so-called "visioning" sessions I attended over the years, there was always a "facilitator" who would pose questions and get responses from the audience. The interaction was always from the facilitator to the individual, from the individual back to the facilitator, then from the facilitator to another individual. So a subtle manipulation was always occurring. This model of interaction is what I call the LEM – Leadership Enhancement Model. It matters not that the facilitator has no vested interest in the results because the leaders who hired this person always control the agenda. The outcome of these visioning sessions is always planned by the leadership ahead of time, and the facilitator is told what issues to raise and what questions to ask. The result is equivalent to developing a wheel with a hub and spokes but no rim. As long as the hub is satisfied with the status quo, it can grow as many spokes as it wants. But if the spokes ever attempt to travel on their own, the wheel, being incomplete, will collapse of its own weight.

Or as Paulo Freire, puts it, with reference to group leaders:

> Our converts…truly desire to transform the unjust order; but because of their background they believe that they must be the executors of the transformation. They talk about the people, but they do not trust them; and trusting the people is the indispensable precondition of revolutionary change.[22]

The Group Enhancement Model. In contrast to the LEM model is what I call the GEM: the Group Enhancement Model. To me, the GEM is a jewel! In this model, the facilitator's role is to solicit input from the residents and promote interchange and cross-referencing. This is a much more difficult technique, with no guaranteed outcome other than a greater appreciation for potential commonality among participants. Nonetheless, the result can be a fully functional and integrated wheel, with a hub, spokes, and an inter-connected and reinforced rim, capable of transporting the community to a better place.

Do groups using the GEM risk losing control over the agenda and the outcome? Absolutely. But many CDCs are willing to take that risk because they know that basic injustice can be remedied with hard work, careful deliberation, and strategic action. These groups have faith that people, once provided with space, information, and the appropriate tools, will make the right choices and manage those choices in a responsible fashion.

These CDCs also believe that problems must be solved by those most affected by those problems – those with a vested interest in the outcome. The reason for this is often lost on well-meaning community leaders. To do something for somebody is to destroy the capacity for that individual to do it on their

---

[22] Paulo Freire, *Pedagogy of the Oppressed,* Continuum Publishing Company, 1970, 1993 p. 42.

The Concept of Community

own. It goes beyond the "teach a man to fish" analogy. In almost every grass roots community development effort that I have been involved in, sooner or later the "leaders" agreed on the need to "do something" to show people that something could be done. The thinking was that if the people were provided with just some concrete example of progress, then they would feel hope and work collectively toward the next desired outcome. However, time and time again, I have seen that this results only in reinforcing the notion that outcomes must come from without (where people have power), and not from within (where people have no power). To see an outcome accomplished without the requisite participation further debilitates those without power.

Top-Down/Bottom-Up. In one memorable instance, the leaders became so frustrated with their inability to "deliver" numbers of people to a City Hall demonstration that they decided that a "bottom-up" organizing approach was untenable and what was needed was a "top-down/bottom-up approach." What they meant was an organizing project that made things happen "from above" while the organizing continued "from below." In other words, the people would organize into a demonstration and the leaders would use the demonstration to negotiate an objective; once the objective was accomplished, the people would see that the demonstration resulted in concrete results; once the people saw the desired outcome, they would seek to be more involved in future actions and the follow-up deliberations.

Those who were motivated to succeed at all costs (judged solely by outcomes achieved) pushed this approach. Those of us who argued that it is disrespectful to define the success of a demonstration by the "numbers of people delivered" (since those people on whose behalf we were working were not cows being delivered to the market) lost the battle. And once the approach to organizing switched in that way, those at the top had license to prescribe the desired outcome and the means towards getting there, leaving it to the organizers to convince people of the righteousness of the cause.

The switch to "top down/bottom up" organizing failed for a number of reasons. It is still the wrong today. As Paulo Freire puts it,

To manipulate is to reify and to reify is to establish a relationship of domestication which may be disguised behind an apparently inoffensive façade.[23]

To fully appreciate this quote, one must appreciate how Freire constantly distinguishes between treating people as "subjects" and treating people as "objects." As a guest lecturer at colleges and universities, I often ask students what they make of this distinction. Very few are able to answer, possibly because grammar is rarely taught in this country, possibly because few are taught to think critically.

Subject-Object. Paulo Freire taught literacy in Brazil. His subject-object analogy referred to the subject and object of a full sentence. The subject is the actor. The subject gets to do things to objects. The objects are passive and without any control. The subject is in total control. The subject has power. The object is powerless and exists to be manipulated. Unfortunately, too many within the field of community development treat people as though they are objects to be manipulated to achieve a desired end. Once people are seen in this way they become "reified" and are ultimately treated no differently than furniture.

I have found in my own work that keeping the subject-object analogy in mind as a working concept helps me ensure that people are not disrespected and that my colleagues and I do not expropriate the effort for our own purposes. This is a useful touchstone to all who work in community development and community organizing. Whenever we engage people in any organizing effort, from the beginning right through the end, we should critique our work and judge its validity based on whether we are treating people like subjects (they are in control and truly are the actors in whatever action is taken) or like objects (we know the issues, we know the answers, and we are essentially filling these objects with the right information and the right actions to be taken).

---

[23] Paulo Freire, *Education for Critical Consciousness*, Continuum International Pub., 1973, p. 149.

IV Community and Neighborhood: Toward a Transformative Model

Any discussion of community development must start with a workable definition of "community." Many of us take the word for granted, assuming that just because people live in a given location, they form a community.[24] But certain additional conditions must exist, the absence of which will cause any sort of community-based initiative to fail.

What is Community? A "community" is a group of people with something in common. But beyond that, for community to exist, there must also be interdependence and the collective capacity to accomplish agreed-upon goals. These three components of community are inextricably linked (and will be discussed at greater length at the end of this chapter). Most so-called "community-building" initiatives assume "community" when only the first of these conditions is in place: commonality. Community builders often see a group of people with a common need or problem and attempt to fix the circumstances through outside intervention and assistance. Most of those engaged in such initiatives ignore the second and third necessary components of a community.

---

[24] For example in Charles Abrams, *The City as Frontier* (Harper & Row, 1965), looking up "community" in the index yields only "See Cities, Neighborhoods, Suburbs."

It is certainly easy to label a group of impoverished people a "community" of people sharing the concerns of every day life and the weight of political circumstances and personal woes. But these people are not a community at all – they are simply an agglomeration of people in similarly depressing circumstances. As Winifred Gallagher notes, "community rests on shared values... and the ability to influence events."[25]

Gallagher did not mention interdependence, yet this is an important feature of community as well. There can be no interdependence between and among people unless there is a need, a capacity, and a recognized self-interest in sharing that capacity. If you need me to fix your roof, I will most likely not do it unless I perceive that some interest of mine is being served. Outside the context of community, my interest would be in receiving payment or some other form of direct reciprocity for my service. But in the context of community, there is an implicit recognition that the community as a whole benefits from the well-being of all its members. As such, considerations of immediate payment and direct reciprocity are irrelevant. All the members of a community perceive themselves as forming one social web – all interconnected, all interdependent and all affected by the individual loss or gain of its members.

So I may help you to fix your roof, but now it is the community as a whole that implicitly owes me something in return for my service. I may never receive anything directly from you in return for having done work for you, but if I never receive anything at all, then I am not really a member of that community. Conversely, you do not owe me anything, but you owe the community as a whole something of value in return. If you never repay the service, then you are undermining the community and eventually will find yourself marginalized or even ostracized.

Community at Risk. I maintain that today "community" as a social, political, and economic construct is deeply threatened. In its place, we have people isolated into individual household units and grouped into geographical clusters.

[25] Winifred Gallagher, *The Power of Place*, Harper Collins, 1993, p. 193.

The inhabitants are linked only through infrastructure and the delivery of local services. Furthermore, these groupings – we generally call them neighborhoods – are totally dependent upon outside economic operations beyond the individual or collective control of those in the neighborhoods.

In the political realm, this transformation of communities into simple neighborhoods operating as externally-dependent, locally-serviced, residential clusters has mirrored the transformation of citizens from active participants in the political life of society into mere taxpayers and consumers of public services. This dismal devolution is a direct function of our economic system, which thrives on individual consumption patterns, workers who are detached from resources needed for production, and citizens who are politically neutered and amenable to manipulation.

This brings us back to the relationship of community and the local economy. In the absence of local economy, there can be no local community, no interdependence, and no collective capacity. And without collective capacity there is no real political capacity.

Community-Building. "Community-building" became widely used in the field of community development in the mid to late-nineties. In 1996, the Chapin Hall Center for Children at the University of Chicago published a compendium of articles on community building.[26] The collection of eight essays and thirty-five responses was intended to provide the best current thinking on the topic. The compendium contained some important insights, such as the recognition that economics was central (even if in an undefined manner) to community-building. Ultimately, however, the book failed for much the same reason that many community-building efforts themselves have failed: the concept of "community" was not sufficiently examined. Community and neighborhood were used as interchangeable terms. The existence of community was pre-

---

[26] Rebecca Stone, Editor, *Core Issues in Comprehensive Community-Building Initiatives,* Chapin Hall Center for Children at the University of Chicago, 1996.

sumed while community-building efforts were being undertaken. But it's impossible to build on something that does not exist.

During the nineties, I became involved in a number of community-building programs. One such effort was funded by the New York Community Trust. It was called the Neighborhood Strategies Project. It became clear to me early on that the foundation's vision of "community-building" was to provide the people of four inner city neighborhoods of New York City with access to jobs and services. The very important breakthrough of this project was its recognition that there is an inextricable link between community and the economy. Its basic flaw was that it sought to superimpose a prescribed construct of community that was similar to the concept of "neighborhood" instead of putting in the necessary work, and risking the possible frustration, of really attempting to build community.

Sectoral Workforce Development. The lead program officer had written a paper on some early efforts at community- building and was enthusiastic about an emerging economic/job development model that focused on a "sectoral" analysis of the local economy. This analysis identified specific economic sectors, such as health care, in which job growth was anticipated. The purpose of the analysis was to determine and project growth areas in the regional economy that local residents might be helped to access. Job training had already been replaced with "workforce development" by the time this initiative started, and a "work first" approach was encouraged. In the end, this "community-building" effort became little more than a job placement program and had very little to do with community-building. It provided some tangible benefit to individuals who took advantage of the opportunities but only limited success overall.

It became clear that the Program Officer from the New York Community Trust, as well as most of the leadership from local community organizations, believed that a productively-functioning community was little more than a geographical area where people have access to living-wage jobs and are provided with life's necessary services. In impoverished areas, the inhabitants should simply be provided with more services. So the sponsors of this effort were hampered by an ill-defined sense of community, confusing it with a well-functioning neighborhood – probably much like the neighborhoods in which the sponsors lived.

The New York Community Trust sponsored several retreats for its leaders. At these retreats, I attempted to challenge the group to better define our goals, both tangible and intangible, and to discuss the concept of community. My efforts clearly exasperated the others.

Bronx Center. Another program with which I became personally involved was called Bronx Center. This effort was initiated by then-Bronx Borough President Fernando Ferrer. For decades, the Bronx had been so devastated that it had become an international symbol of urban decay. In Italy, there was an area of Milan known as the "Bronx of Milan," because of its physical condition. In France, there was an expression, "C'est quoi se Bronx?" referring to any situation that was out of control and beyond any rational resolution.

Ultimately, the Bronx was revived as a result of substantial public subsidies, an extensive infrastructure of community development corporations, and local leadership that focused on results and not on patronage. Fernando Ferrer was a key player in this revival; he set the tone for the borough from the top. Having seen to the Bronx's revival, he sought to create the equivalent of a Bronx downtown. Unlike Brooklyn or Manhattan, the Bronx had never been its own city, so it did not have a downtown area. Ferrer's vision was to exploit and further develop different "development nodes" of closely-grouped health, recreational, educational and commercial facilities and to connect these nodes to provide the equivalent of a downtown.

He also sought to capitalize on the public investment that was scheduled, over the next ten years through the city's capital budget, to maximize the benefit to the borough. First, his office worked with the Regional Plan Association to write a report which provided much of the platform for the Bronx Center planning effort. Following the publication of that report, Ferrer convened a group of leaders under the leadership of Richard Kahan, a former power broker who headed the Battery Park City Authority and New York State's Urban Development Corporation (later renamed the Empire State Development Corporation). Kahan was and is very well connected, and he demands that public servants spend taxpayer money to advance the general welfare – and do it in a way that is measurable and accountable. (His no-nonsense approach is probably the reason why he is not in government today and has not succeeded in his limited forays into elective office.) A steering committee was established to coordinate the ambitious planning effort, consisting of the Bronx Borough President's office, Pratt Center, the Municipal Art Society, Urban Assembly, and the Parodneck Foundation.

The Bronx Center initiative began with a flurry. Public announcements were made. Local forums were held – one attended by then HUD Secretary Jack Kemp. Development opportunities were targeted around areas of opportunity and planned public investment. The area around Yankee Stadium and the Bronx Terminal Market was seen as potentially providing a Bronx version of Camden Yards. The waterfront, mostly inaccessible due to industrial use and the existence of a commuter rail line, was analyzed and designed for eventual passive and active recreational use. The area around Hostos College and Lincoln Hospital was viewed as having potential for biotechnology companies.

The area east of Yankee Stadium, where a new and huge criminal court was being planned, was analyzed for uses that would be neighborhood-friendly. Commercial space would be directly accessed from sidewalks as opposed to behind fortress-type walls. Various projects would benefit the neighborhood. Plans were put in place for a local charter school for law and justice to encourage the area's youth to pursue careers in criminal justice. This offered hope for the young people in the community, in direct contrast to some of the negative, even if inadvertent, signals being sent to our youth.

The Ultimate Irony. At this time, I was teaching a class at the Graduate School of Planning and Architecture at Columbia University. My students were working on a planning project for Bronx Center and happened upon a sign that was replete with irony. As was the city's practice, all capital projects were announced through site signs that would read something like, "Rebuilding the future of the Bronx," and then list the names of the Mayor and other elected officials. The particular site in question was the site of a new juvenile detention facility to be built on 149th Street, just east of the HUB commercial district and right across the street from a public school. So this site, the future home of a juvenile prison, also had one of these signs lauding the use of public funds in "Rebuilding" the Bronx – in full view of the junior high school students who may have been looking out of their class windows and pondering their futures.

Surely establishing a charter school offering a more positive entry into the criminal justice system was a more hopeful idea.

Melrose Commons. Another major component of the planning effort came out of the RPA planning exercise, which focused on the re-development of the Melrose Commons Urban Renewal Area. Under the RPA plan, the Melrose Urban renewal area was to be razed and replaced with mid-rise multiple dwellings for moderate and middle income residents. When I asked then deputy Borough President, Genevieve Brooks, about the current residents of the area and how they felt about the plan, her response was something like, "nobody lives there and those that do want to move." This seemed to me highly improbable, but I held my tongue.

Ferrer and Kahan both initially endorsed the Melrose Commons urban renewal plan – as well as endorsing a planning process that was open, inclusive and subject to review by residents. Out of this endorsed approach came the creation of the Bronx Community Forum, which I chaired. The Forum became the outreach and resident participation component to the planning effort.

The Bronx Community Forum held its first meeting at Lincoln Hospital one Saturday morning to describe the Melrose Commons plan and get some local feedback. We expected an orderly meeting, but it was soon disrupted by residents of Melrose who lambasted the plan and accused the Borough President and others of conspiring with the police to remove them from their homes.

I often cite this meeting when speaking about community organizing and the importance of understanding perspective. After this meeting, many of the

Bronx Center sponsors and leaders felt that since the charges (that there was an organized conspiracy between Ferrer and the police department) were demonstrably false, the people making them were fools. However, from the perspective of those living and working in the Melrose area, their conclusions (even though wrong) were a reasonable derivative of the circumstances they confronted daily, such as open and aggressive drug dealing while official enforcement agencies focused mainly on less dramatic quality of life infractions, such as traffic violations, and unclean sidewalks, which targeted otherwise law-abiding citizens and businesses. Once we "knew where they were coming from," it was possible to understand the residents' complaints and address them respectfully.

Following that tumultuous meeting, I toured the area with a volunteer planner for Bronx Center, Petr Stand, to meet local homeowners. We began to hold regular Tuesday forums at a local church and Petr, assisted by Lee Weintraub and in conjunction with the Urban Assembly and Pratt Center, started a planning studio where the initial urban renewal plan was changed block by block. In the end, the leadership of Bronx Center, including Fernando Ferrer, approved our new, minimally disruptive, contextual urban renewal plan. As a result, the original displacement urban renewal plan was scrapped. This new plan went on to be approved and is still being implemented as of this writing.

The End of Bronx Center. As a community-building effort, the Bronx Center initiative gets an A for effort. This project was a major planning effort that sought to make the billions of dollars of planned public investment benefit the residents. It was a great idea, promoted by well-meaning, well-connected, hardworking, and highly intelligent people. However, in the end, the effort was built on public resources and was doomed to fail once those resources dried up, as they did with a change in city administrations. In 1989, David Dinkins lost the mayoralty to Rudolph Giuliani, who ultimately defunded most of the Bronx Center program initiatives.

Bronx Center did result in a few concrete results: a revised Melrose Commons urban renewal plan, a new school, and some solid planning for future work. However, as a community-building effort, it failed first and foremost because it was an attempt to infuse community into a planning initiative.

And even before the money was gone, sponsors and leaders of the project became engaged in bitter feuds arising from the lack of planning and consensus-building and what we meant by certain basic terms.

Community Building Today. Two prevailing forms of community building are currently practiced. The first I would define as a "static enhancement model." This form of community-building reinforces current power relationships, seeking only to enhance the capacity of individuals to deal more effectively with prevailing circumstances. In this model, the current circumstances are assumed to be immutable and the product of natural forces (the "invisible hand," if you will).

Most community-building initiatives subscribe to the static-enhancement model, just as their funders do. This model prescribes aid to the needy in a manner that does not threaten the funders' world view and comfortable existence. Such sponsors believe that the "less fortunate" only lack information, access, training, values, and positive role models in order to succeed. Failure is due to these individual deficiencies. These sponsors believe that for the poor to get ahead, they must overcome personal and local barriers to gain entry into the mainstream. Programs and funding streams are organized around these assumptions.

But conditions are not immutable. Change is constant. Change occurs without pause and the only questions really are:

1. will we adapt to change?
2. will we be buried by it?
3. will we ourselves become agents of change?

As for the "natural order" of things as applying to human affairs, I believe that Isaiah Berlin is instructive:

...ends are not, as had been thought for more than two millennia, objective values, discoverable within man or in a transcendent realm by some special faculty. Ends are not discovered at all, but made, not found but created...There are no objective rules, only what we make.[27]

In the static-enhancement model of community-building, there is an assumption that people's problems stem from the wrong attitude and a lack of information, education, training and access. It is assumed that with proper adjustments in these areas individuals will become productive members of society.

In my view, such an assumption is ridiculous. An approach that views economic marginalization, political disenfranchisement, and individual disempowerment as totally dependent upon individual dysfunctions is either naïve or simply asserted for institutional or political expediency. Such a view sees poverty as pathology – a condition that must be analyzed, treated, and, when not capable of remediation, managed, institutionally isolated, or punished. In short, the static-enhancement model of community-building has nothing to do with community at all. It has everything to do with the question that has plagued those in power since the French Revolution – what to do about the poor?

The Transformative Model. In contrast to the static-enhancement model of community-building, there is the transformative model of community-building. This approach views external circumstances as playing a central role in creating area-wide social, economic, and political dependencies. Within this view, community-building efforts seek to organize residents in ways that rebuild meaningful relationships between them. These meaningful connections then redefine a sense of collective identity, place, and capacity. Within this paradigm, the institutional sponsor is not viewed as caretaker, or manager, but as facilitator in a process that leads to the proper relationship between itself and the residents or community members served (as opposed to the sponsor servicing clients). Further, the institution then serves as a vehicle to implement locally-generated action plans. In other words, at the successful end of the proc-

---

[27] Isaiah Berlin, *The Crooked Timber of Humanity,* Alfred A. Knopf, 1991, pp. 227-228.

ess, the relationship among residents will change, as will the relationship between residents and their local institutions. If a local institution refuses to accommodate this transformation, that institution must be replaced or displaced by another, accountable community institution.

As an example of a transformative model, assume that a group of residents decides that there are talents, capacities and needs within the group that can be addressed through mutual aid and cooperation. All the members of the group have some free time. The different members of the group have: access to a vehicle and the ability to drive, the ability to cook, baby-sit, house-watch, supervise latch-key kids, knit, research, word process, perform home repairs, and so on. They decide to set up some form of cooperative arrangement. And utilizing a system for documenting the contributions and receipts of each member of the cooperative (i.e. establishing their own currency or method of bookkeeping), the members begin to offer and receive goods and services from within this closed economic system.

By creating this form of cooperative arrangement, the members of this cooperative have formed a community. This community, as all communities, is not totally self-contained and self-sufficient, but it does serve the economic needs of its members. This community is based upon commonality. Due to the diverse array of talents, interdependence has developed. Since each member has a contribution to make, collectively the cooperative group has the capacity to achieve desired outcomes – even if the outcome is that each family is a bit more economically sufficient and less economically marginalized.

Through this effort, a transformation has occurred. Relations among the members of the community have been transformed. And, in some small way, this internal transformation can create a new power dynamic that affects the broader scheme of existing power-sharing processes and institutional arrangements. If this community decides to address some broader concern such as neighborhood security, or the educational enhancement of their children, they will be in a better position to create an institutional response as well as the ability to hold the institution accountable.

The Bodega Conundrum. It is important not to confuse the concepts of neighborhood and community. Neighborhoods are "a collection of people and institutions occupying a spatially defined area."[28] Physical proximity to each other creates neighbors and neighborhoods. People reside in neighborhoods as long as each person, most often dependent upon employment and other income sources from outside the area, can afford to live there – or until they choose to "buy up" into a better neighborhood, or are forced to leave due to a change in natural or political circumstances (i.e. urban renewal and eminent domain).

The more affluent the neighborhood is, the more diverse and numerous the services are, at least up through the upper middle class, beyond which amenities are most often self-contained through private employment of drivers and caretakers, use of country clubs for enjoyment of open space and recreational activities, use of private education, private facilities and the like. The poorer the neighborhood, the less diverse the services, such as inner city neighborhoods which have a *bodega* (a Spanish deli) on every corner.

When I first moved to the South Bronx in 1976, I wondered why there were so many bodegas. Over time I realized that ten acres in Scarsdale and ten acres in the South Bronx may have the same aggregate purchasing power but the difference is that in the South Bronx there are more people per acre with less money per household so that all they can buy are the basics. It seems a simple enough concept, but took a while for me to figure out.

However, there are problems with this theory. Why did older ghettos have more retail diversity, with the same density and perhaps even less aggregate household income (or, in economic terms, aggregate demand)? Formerly, poor neighborhoods of New York City had considerable retail diversity, i.e. the butcher, the baker, etc. This diversity was possible due to the economic multiplier effect that was more prevalent in the late 19th and early 20th centuries than

---

[28] *Social Capital and Poor Communities* (Russell Sage Foundation, 2001), edited by Saegert, Thompson, Warren. See Chapter Four, *Crime and Public Safety*, by Robert J. Sampson, p. 90, making reference to Robert Park (1916), *The City: Suggestions for the Investigations of Human Behavior in the Urban Environment.*

it is today. If a low-income person spends a dollar on bread and the shopkeeper takes the money home to Scarsdale, then the dollar is spent just one time in the low income neighborhood and then is gone. However, if a low income person buys bread, and the shopkeeper takes that dollar and repairs his shoes, and if the cobbler takes that dollar and gets a hair cut, and it all happens in the same neighborhood, the neighborhood benefits from the multiplier effect. So it is possible to have retail diversity within a low income neighborhood. But if there is no substantial multiplier effect because there is no integrated local economy, then you get a bodega on every block.

Some would disagree with this analysis. Grogan and Proscio, for example, make the case that the inner city has more density of purchasing power and therefore can accommodate more retail business. However, their evidence for this comes from neighborhoods where purchasing power has been increased by working class families living in newly constructed and heavily subsidized homes, thus allowing them more disposable income.

The Jacobs Prescription. Of course, some neighborhoods function better than others. Jane Jacobs lists a number of variables that make for a functional urban neighborhood. She takes the position that a functional urban neighborhood must have diversity and that this diversity is a function of a number of factors, namely, mixed primary uses, small blocks, "aged buildings" (along with more modern ones), and concentration.[29]

Mixed primary uses mean that there are different activities at different times of the day. For example, residents may use the sidewalks and retail businesses mostly in the early morning, evening and weekends. During the day, workers at a manufacturing facilities or offices put money into the community during breaks and lunch hour. On holidays and weekends, when plants and offices may be closed, the neighborhood may attract tourists. This mixture of activities makes a neighborhood thrive.

---

[29] Jane Jacobs, *The Death and Life of Great American Cities*, Vintage Books (Alfred A. Knoff, Inc. and Random House, Inc.) 1961, chapters 7 through 12.

Jacobs emphasizes the importance of short city blocks. She maintains that long blocks force pedestrians along cavernous routes, while shorter blocks allow for a variety of paths to reach an intended destination. These various paths allow exposure to more people and more businesses.

Aged buildings are needed beside modern ones to allow for housing choices among a mix of residents of different economic classes and walks of life. When these people walk the streets and use the neighborhood stores, they do so as equals. This kind of equality, Jacobs maintains, is essential to a neighborhood. When a stockbroker and a shoe shiner go to the store and each spends his loose change for a newspaper, they are both "equal" to that task. This equality paves the way for other neighborly activities and manifestations (such as collective security).

Jacobs also makes a good case for concentration as a necessary component of a healthy neighborhood. She states that though concentration is generally viewed as essential for downtown areas, the "relationship between concentration and diversity is very little considered when it comes to city districts where residence is the chief use."[30]

Jacobs makes the distinction between concentration as a necessary component of a healthy neighborhood, and overcrowding, which is not.

> Densities are too low or too high when they frustrate city diversity instead of abetting it.[31]

Neighborhood vs. Community. Note that some professionals in the field of environmental psychology have a different understanding of "neighborhood." Robert Gifford writes, "Neighborhoods are cognitive creations, not geographical entities."[32]

I agree that a neighborhood is not a fixed geographical entity and that it can shift over time and in relation to shifting human interactions and interrelation-

---

[30] Jacobs, J. Op. cit., p. 201.
[31] *Ibid*, p.209.
[32] Robert Gifford, *Environmental Psychology, Principles & Practices*, Allyn & Bacon, 1997, p.20.

The Concept of Community

ships. However, a neighborhood is originally geographically based because people are geographically based. Over time, a location such as Little Italy in lower Manhattan may shift from a functioning neighborhood to a block or two of restaurants and, eventually, to nothing other than a state of mind. But that is not to say that Little Italy was never anything more than a "cognitive creation."

A neighborhood can function, and function well, without community. But economically-thriving, diverse, socially agreeable neighborhoods do not a community make. Neighborhoods cannot be communities where there is no interdependence, no collective control over the resources necessary to achieve common goals, and no sense of shared commonality beyond proximity, class, and a shared right to demand services that are purchased through private dollars or that are made possible through local tax levy authority.

The Three Components of Community.

1. Commonality. Something that a group of people hold in common is a necessary basis for community. This common element might be geographical circumstances, shared concerns and values, children, beliefs, needs, issues, etc. But although commonality is a necessary component of community, it is only one such element and not the only basis for community organizing efforts. Without a more expansive perspective, most such efforts will fail once the external supports are removed.
2. Interdependence. This is a difficult concept to appreciate, especially for those who fund comprehensive community initiatives, community-building, and community organizing efforts. What interdependence presumes is that a necessary component of community is economic. In my experience, since the funders and the policy-makers (many of whom believe they have all the answers) start with the premise that the world is as it is because of the natural order of things, the goal then becomes to teach people how to survive and thrive within this world that, after all, works so well for them. But let any one of them lose their household incomes and find themselves without the benefit of family or inherited

wealth, they will learn soon enough that the "community" in which they believe they live is not a community at all, just a local residential service cluster that sustains them only to the extent that it is supported by them through their outside economic endeavors. "Community," without some economic capacity that defines the relations between and among its members and advances the quality of life of those within that "community," is not a community at all, just an aggregation of people within some set of shared circumstances.

3. Collective Capacity. This third necessary component of community follows from the first two components – commonality and interdependence. For a community to be a community there must be an internal capacity to accomplish goals that are necessary or desirable. Collective capacity results from each individual having something to offer to the collective "pot" from which common good can be achieved. In established communities, the vehicles for accomplishing the commonly held agenda of its members are institutions such as local civic clubs, associations, concerned citizen committees and the like. I would maintain that it is possible to gauge the health of any community by determining the extent to which its institutions are controlled by the residents or by outsiders.

With regard to impoverished neighborhoods, ask yourself the question: with no access to the primary sources of wealth (natural resources, information, technology, means of production) and with most people trending towards negative wealth, what opportunity is there for residents to exercise power and form a true community? This is the topic of the next chapter.

V **Empowerment**

What does "empowerment" mean in the context of community development? Ron Shiffman describes empowerment as the

> ability to make informed choices and to have the social, political, and economic capability of meaningfully contributing to the realization of those choices.[33]

This may seem like a good working definition of the term, but the "ability to make informed choices" begs the question of who frames those choices to begin with. Take our electoral choices. As citizens living in a democratic society, we have the right to choose who will represent us. However, those choices are most often screened for appropriateness by those already in power, making a mockery out of the electoral process.

Furthermore, to have the "social, political, and economic capability of meaningfully contributing" begs the question of the relative weight of different contributions. If a community development corporation sees itself as the disseminator of information and the framer of acceptable choices from which residents choose, then when all is said and done, Shiffman's definition is based on a political model that sees power as being granted by those who have it to

---

[33] Ronald Shiffman, "Comprehensive and Integrative Planning for Community Development," A Discussion Paper for the Community Economic Development Study Conference Research Center, New School for Social Research, June 14, 1989 (www.picced.org/advocacy/compplan.htm).

those who do not have it. This is accomplished in most community settings by providing local residents with the space, resources, tools and general framework to permit managed access to political issues so as to "empower" the local community. But power cannot be granted. Anyone who attempts to do so is not granting power but rather is granting authority that can be withdrawn or amended at whim.

Power and Community. Hannah Arendt's definition of power is more useful:

> In distinction to strength, which is the gift and the possession of every man in his isolation against all other men, power comes into being only if and when men join themselves together for the purpose of action, and it will disappear when, for whatever reason, they disperse and desert one another. Hence, binding and promising, combining and covenanting are the means by which power is kept in existence…[34]

Power is derived. It is generated by the deliberations and actions of men and women who join together to collectively address some common concern. People can collectively develop power in and of themselves, but power cannot be *given* to them. A further point can be inferred by Arendt's definition of power. In the absence of community there is no power. As a corollary, the existence of community presumes power.

Power, like democracy, is never self-sustaining. It must be constantly practiced; otherwise it disappears. But does it really disappear? In the absence of community, it does. Individuals endowed with resources (personal capability, access to human and natural resources, information, technology, etc.) can join together for some common enterprise and exercise power. For that period of time during which the common enterprise is undertaken, a community does exist (commonality, interdependence and collective capacity). But once the mutual enterprise is exhausted, the community disappears, along with the power it generated, and must be re-negotiated anew each time a mutual enterprise is undertaken.

---

[34] Hannah Arendt, *On Revolution*, Penguin, 1990, p. 175.

In a healthy ongoing community, there is already a connection among its members. There is no need to join together for the purpose of accomplishing some goal since they are already joined together. Within an established and functioning community, power never really disappears but rather goes dormant and can be revived at any time.

Of course, there is no such thing as an absolute community (totally independent in and of itself), and there is certainly no such thing as absolute power within a community. Any community necessarily operates within a larger social, economic, and political context and operates as a recognized component of that larger society's power-sharing arrangements.

The Liberated Man. In order to have collective capacity, there must be individual capacity. Individual capacity allows us to contribute something of value to a collective purpose. This "something" might be time, talent, direct service, advice, moral support, inspiration, goods, money or other means of support for a common effort. Something must be contributed to the common cause from our private selves. In ancient Greece, for example, a "liberated" man was a man (there was, of course, no concept of a liberated woman) who had productive land and sufficient domestic labor to take care of all of life's basic needs. Therefore, the liberated man had time and the capacity to engage in public affairs. The political community was comprised of liberated men who had the luxury of engaging in public affairs because their basic necessities were taken care of. The situation is similar today. Only the rich or those sponsored by the rich have easy access to electoral politics because the rest of us are too busy struggling to maintain an ever-higher standard of living.

Where does this leave regular people in their relation to effective communities (with the power to accomplish shared goals)? From a perspective of power, they are no better than the servants of Plato who had to labor incessantly simply to provide for their own sustenance – and that of Plato. If there is nothing to offer community, can there be any capacity to become a part of a community? Can there be any basis for the exercise of power?

Of course, in modern times people do have spare time. Indeed, many who are not employed have far too much of it, but this time is absorbed by distractions based upon societal demands for individual consumption, dealt with later in this work. It is also spent talking. And assuming that the discussion moves beyond "American Idol" contestants, Anna Nicole Smith, and who among Leslie Lohan, Britney Spears, and Paris Hilton is the biggest public embarrassment, it is possible that whenever two people come together and discuss a common problem, they are creating "public space," and they are engaging in political dialogue. Anything is now possible.

A Common Confusion. Too often in community development work, outsiders confuse local institutions as being the very communities they purport to represent. This is particularly true when the leader of such an institution is indigenous to the area. Instead of being community institutions, however, too often they merely fill the void left by an absence of community. To find examples of institutions that fill the void of community as opposed to serving community, one has only to look at any inner city area. Local institutions abound, institutions that are funded and accountable to outside agencies and organizations. In essence, they are paid to manage poor people through the allocation of inadequate public supports. These local organizations will speak eloquently about their "community" and their work to benefit the "members" of the local "community." But in most of these areas there is no community, at least not with respect to the institution claiming one, and there is no power, only authority granted to the local institution from without – again, revocable authority.

Take, for example, two "community-building" projects discussed in other sections of this book, which operated in the South Bronx in the nineties: the Community Comprehensive Revitalization Program (CCRP), funded by the SURDNA Foundation, and the Neighborhood Strategies Project (NSP), funded by the New York Community Trust. In both these efforts the emphases was placed on local institutional development to enhance local capacity so that these local institutions could deliver comprehensive services to residents more effectively and efficiently.

Under the NSP project, new collaborations of existing social services organizations and new implementing entities were funded and developed to provide targeted employment services to residents. But this was far from any semblance of "building community," as the project was originally billed. Additionally, when the funding ended ("authority revoked"), so did the new entities created by the initiative.

As for CCRP, existing CDCs were tapped for this new initiative that provided new funds for very extravagant local planning exercises and enhanced social services. But these planning exercises were dominated by local institutional leaders and the primary role of residents was to attend "visioning" sessions, respond to a pre-determined set of questions, and participate in case-managed health realization exercises. Throughout, CCRP was billed and described as a "Comprehensive Community Initiative." The thinking behind it was that housing groups needed to expand their capacity beyond housing development and operation to include a wider array of social services: economic development, job development, career counseling, and educational/literacy training. In this way, the housing developed by local CDCs would have a greater chance of surviving with residents who were themselves successful citizens.

Contrast the above to the Melrose Commons planning initiative mentioned elsewhere in this book. Space was provided. Information was disseminated to the residents. A local organizer, Sandra Colon, was assigned to the community – not to manage a pre-determined outcome, but to facilitate deliberative dialogue among residents. People were given the opportunity to connect to their issues; to appreciate that these issues were shared by others (and were not merely private troubles); to join with others and to come up with a plan to work together for a common cause – defeating the original Melrose Commons Urban Renewal Plan and creating a new, acceptable plan. The Nos Quedamos/We Stay Committee was established as the community institution to work for this common goal.

To my mind, this was a very successful "community-building" exercise. I was the convener and facilitator of the initial planning phases, and far from having "revocable authority" over this initiative, it was *the residents who re-*

moved me from a leadership position! (This was appropriate since I had no vested interest in the outcome.)

Action. No discussion of power can be complete without a discussion of "action." In the Arendt quote above, power was described as the joining together of people for the purpose of taking action. Talk without action is nothing but empty rhetoric. Action without deliberation is nothing but hollow activism. "Power is actualized only where word and deed have not parted company."[35] This precondition of power – deliberation and action, or praxis, was also a central theme for Paulo Freire in his life's works. In his discussion of liberation of oppressed people, deliberation and action were critical.

> Liberation is a praxis: the action and reflection of men and women upon their world in order to transform it.[36]

A group of people can "empower" themselves, but no third party can "empower" another person or group of people. However, an outside party can facilitate the process, support the process, and participate in the process of empowerment, as in the Melrose Commons example just cited. Here there was room for continued participation by planning experts, architects, traffic consultants, environmental consultants, elected officials, and funders in a cooperative effort to work directly with local residents in the redevelopment of their plan and the future of their community.

---

[35] Arendt, H. *The Human Condition,* Op. cit., p. 200.
[36] Freire, P. *Pedagogy of the Oppressed,* Op. cit., p. 60.

VII Politics and Democracy

> Politics everywhere is essentially the art of buying votes with other people's money, typically by collecting taxes from a large group of faceless people and turning the money over to a small group of people whose faces are well known at election time.[37]

The cynicism behind this view is well-founded. Candidates are chosen for their fund-raising skills rather than their ability to govern. Most citizens discharge their civic duties by merely casting periodic votes. But political participation does not have to be so narrowly defined.

I describe politics much more broadly. Political involvement can begin as simply as two or more people coming together, deliberating, and resolving to act upon current power arrangements in such a manner as to attempt to transform those arrangements for their mutual benefit. Take, for example, the Tillman family who insisted on learning the truth about their son's death in Afghanistan. Originally billed as a hero felled by enemy fire, Captain Pat Tillman's death was in fact the result of "friendly fire," and the military purposefully used Tillman's fame as a former football star to advance Bush's political propaganda. The family refused to accept the lie, even though it placed their son in a noble light, and sought the truth through the media and through

---

[37] John Tierney, "Our Children are Losers?" *The New York Times*, February 12, 2002.

Congressional oversight authority. Ultimately, the truth did not topple the Bush administration, but it certainly disrupted political arrangements, helping to shift political power from the executive branch to the legislative branch and giving new weight to the media, veteran's groups, and peace groups.

The Tillman example is somewhat unusual in that shifting political winds made it somewhat easier for the Tillman family to effect a change. Political disenfranchisement and disempowerment is closer to the norm for vast numbers of American citizens, and this lack of political power is directly related to the loss of local economy and the loss of local community. Citizens have become little more than consumers of government services who, when upset about the quality of what they have "purchased" with their votes and their taxes, simply switch brands. Without community, the political character of citizens is reduced to one act, voting. This is simply not enough for the long-term sustenance of a democratic society.

Reviving Political Power. To revive political power, it is necessary to decide on the primary focal point for the generation of power. In a democracy, that focal point is supposed to be the people. However, democracy can be formal without being substantive, and this transformation (what C. Wright Mills refers to as the "debilitation of the public") can happen over time and almost without notice. Mills describes the results of this political debilitation as one in which citizens

> lose their will for decisions because they do not possess the instruments for decision; they lose their sense of political belonging because they do not belong; they lose their political will because they do not see a way to realize it.[38]

The philosopher John Dewey once referred to politics as "the shadow cast upon society by big business." That may also seem like a cynical view. But when you think about how discussions are framed and who gets the opportu-

---

[38] C. Wright Mills, *Power, Politics & People,* The Collected Essays of C. Wright Mills, Ed. Irving Louis Horowitz, Oxford University Press (1963), *The Structure of Power in American Society* (1958), page 37.

nity to frame the debate, it would appear that in a society dominated by economic considerations on a mass-producing, mass-consuming scale, politics *is* the shadow cast upon society by business – the seemingly dominant interest to which all other interests are subordinate.

To cite one example – health care. Poll after poll demonstrates that most citizens prefer a simplified, universal form of health care modeled after Medicare. But prior to the Democratic run-up to the 2008 Presidential election, the insurance and pharmaceutical companies have been calling the shots and framing the "anti-socialized medicine" debate, which hopefully reached its nadir when President Bush claimed that poor people already have universal care – through hospital emergency rooms!

The Misnomer, "Public Hearings." In our democracy, politics has taken on extravagant form with little popular substance. I cannot remember how many "public hearings" I have attended over the years. Each hearing is documented, and at the end of the hearing there are large volumes of paper representing the "record." But few times have I ever seen the relevant elected or appointed officials actually in attendance at a public hearing. Once I testified before a New York City Council committee and asked if there were any elected officials among of those sitting at the dais, a dais occupied by seemingly disaffected individuals who were mostly on the phone, having conversations with each other, and even eating lunch. There wasn't even one.

That is why most public hearings are misnamed. They are really only "public speakings," since everyone gets to speak, but no one really has to listen. The point is to produce a record that can be trotted out in a court of law to demonstrate the breadth of consideration that was given to the opinions of the people – even if the decision-making had already been made before the public hearing.

Democrats and Aristocrats. The argument over whether and how the people should rule these United States is hundreds of years old. For Thomas Jefferson, the people were to be trusted with political decision-making, even at the risk of making mistakes. He distinguished between a democrat, a person who has faith in people and their ability to deliberate and decide public matters, and an aristocrat, a person who operates in elite groupings that have the burden of making public decisions and then telling the people what is good for them.

The Democratic Ideal. A very positive view of democracy was expressed in John Dewey's book, published about 60 years ago, *The Problems of Men*:

> The keynote of democracy as a way of life may be expressed... as the necessity for the participation of every mature human being in the formation of values that regulate the living of men together: which is necessary from the standpoint of both the general welfare and the full development of human beings as individuals.[39]

Unfortunately, this democratic ideal, which we cherish in slogans, songs, testimonials, has become further from popular grasp as people become more isolated, more economically marginalized and, as a result, politically disenfranchised. But there is a strong argument, and stronger historical precedent, to suggest that if a person is not political, that person is not free. In the words of Professor J. Peter Euben:

> To be political is to be free and visa versa, because it is in the realm of politics that people unite to constitute a human world, to empower each other in order to jointly take control and responsibility for forces that might otherwise control them.[40]

Representative Democracy. To me, any form of "representative democracy" is in itself a contradiction in terms. Political participation must be directly undertaken to be effective and meaningful. When we speak of democracy in terms of popular participation in democratic politics, we must speak about it from a local, community perspective because that is where people live, play, and raise families.

---

[39] John Dewey, "Problems of Men," as cited in Floyd Hunter, *Community Power Structure*, The University of North Carolina Press, 1953, p. 234.
[40] J. Peter Euben, *Democracy in America: Bringing it all Back Home,* Kettering Foundation (1993)

As political decision-making has become more remote from the everyday life of the common person, historians and commentators have felt the need to justify our system as still being a popular democracy. Social scientists have expended entire careers expounding upon why we still live in a democracy even as the connection between citizens' input and public outcomes becomes more and more attenuated. They have come up with several theories.

The Process Theory of Democracy. In this theory, democracy is expressed through professionalized and political decision-makers. This power to exercise political control is acquired by individuals who compete against one another through the electoral process. Here, there is no illusion that allows the common good to be played out in the marketplace of competing ideas. Whoever wins gets to exercise power. Of course, this political process is still viewed as democratic since it is posited that if those in power are not obedient to those who elected them, they will be thrown out of office.

Joseph Schumpeter was an advocate of this theory.[41] He believed it so ardently that throughout the seventies he thought our political process would eventually lead to socialism. He believed that the majority would grow tired of the economic struggle and would politically opt to redistribute wealth through the democratic process the people purportedly controlled. Of course, this has not happened.

The Group Theory of Democracy. Under the group theory of democracy, espoused by David Truman,[42] democracy is expressed politically through groups that are tempered, disciplined and implicitly threatened by two factors:
1. "potential groups" that may form to compete directly with them if they lose touch, and

---

[41] See Joseph A. Schumpeter, *Can Capitalism Survive?*, Harper & Row, 1978.
[42] David Truman, *The Government Process: Political Interests and Public Opinion* (1951). See David Ricci, *Community Power and Democratic Theory: The Logic of Political Analysis*, Random House (1971).

2. "overlapping memberships" that will ensure that diversity is the norm and that no one group can rule.

Truman's point is that as new needs arise and new social and economic arrangements are made, new political groups are formed which act upon the political process. Are these groups primarily acting upon the formal processes of our political system? If so, who is engaged in substantive political decision-making? What are the underlying assumptions of the society as a whole that lend themselves to this kind of tension and reconciliation benefiting all segments of society? And finally, who is to say that the groups themselves are not co-opted and part of the ruling class?

The Pluralistic Theory of Democracy. In the nineteen fifties, Robert Dahl promoted a theory that assumes that most citizens are simply not interested in politics.[43] He posits that nothing can be done to change that. However, we still live in a democracy because, according to Dahl, there is a political stratum within which the "political man" functions. This stratum of society is comprised of diverse people representing every interest group in the country: political groups, pressure groups, lobbyists, civic associations and more. The intensity of activity assures that all are represented. According to Dahl, democracy is also ensured through what he calls "slack political power." For example, if cigarette advertising in stores frequented by youth becomes recognized as a problem, a group of parents and children's advocates may join together in a new coalition to lobby Congress for new advertising restraints on cigarette companies. Theoretically, this new group would only need to be created if an existing group was not sufficiently willing to take up the cause. Through "slack political power," the new group is created, and through its work it becomes a new player, attempting to solve the problem through new legislation, regulations, or enforcement.

---

[43] Robert Dahl, *Who Governs? Democracy and Power in an American City* (1958). See David Ricci, *Community Power and Democratic Theory: The Logic of Political Analysis,* Random House (1971).

Of course, anyone who objectively views the lobbying industry today sees what kinds of groups (mostly trade associations and industrial lobbies) get the attention of elected and appointed officials. The average citizen is not represented at all.

The "Understructure" of Society. Social scientists such as Floyd Hunter believed that every community is maintained by the many but that power to change is in the hands of a few. The elites make the major decisions. What he referred to as the "understructure" of society maintains the system. The population for the most part is kept in check by the need for credit and employment. Furthermore, the news and entertainment media helps convert active citizens into passive consumers. This, in effect, makes the average citizen politically sterile.[44] According to this view, the role of the public, the "ignorant and meddlesome outsiders," as Walter Lippman facetiously called them, is to be "spectators" not "participants," who show up every couple of years to ratify decisions made elsewhere or to select among representatives of dominant sectors in what's called an election.[45]

Elites Aligned. C. Wright Mills took the "elitist" theory of politics much further, claiming that the elite members of society (political, industrial and military) are really of one mind because their interests are fundamentally aligned. Those within this category have the capacity to cross sectors readily, leading to what he called the "governmentalization of the lobby". The hiring of corporate or military advocates into public service allows them to affect desired private sector outcomes from within the public sector. Mills believed that American society was slowly transforming from a society of "publics" to a "mass society" where competition goes on "between the crowd of manipulators with their

---

[44] Floyd Hunter, *Community Power Structure*, The University of North Carolina Press, 1953.
[45] Noam Chomsky, *Keeping the Rabble in Line,* Common Courage Press, 1994, p. 243.

mass media." And he believed that the "issues that now shape man's fate are neither raised nor decided by any public at large."[46]

Republican President Eisenhower, as he was leaving office, warned against the potential threat to democracy posed by the aligned elites.

> In the councils of government, we must guard against the acquisition of unwarranted influence, whether sought or unsought, by the military industrial complex. The potential for the disastrous rise of misplaced power exists and will persist.

With this 1961 speech, Eisenhower, of all people, coined the term "the military industrial complex."

Democracy Betrayed? The Charter Revision of 1989. Most of my experience in the political realm has taken place in New York City. My role can be viewed as falling under Robert Dahl's "pluralistic" theory of democracy. During the 1989 New York City Charter Revision deliberations, for instance, there was a small group of advocates who would appear at just about every hearing. Besides myself, there were Marcy Benstock of the Clean Air Campaign, Bonnie Brower of the Association of Neighborhood and Housing Development, Sam Sue and Eddie Bautista from New York Lawyers for Pubic Interest, Marie Dormuth of Chelsea, and a handful of others. This group of gadflies (who were once members of the much larger group, Citizens for Charter Change, chaired by then-Councilmember Ruth Messinger) went by no name and worked hard to make certain changes in the charter.

The problem was that Charter Revision was very complicated. Additionally, the Charter Revision Commission was well-funded, and they did a superb job of selling their recommendations, including colorful inserts in the Sunday editions of the city's major dailies. Furthermore, the progressive sector in New York City split on the issue after Ruth Messinger met with the Chairman of the

---

[46] The quotes by Mills are from his essays, "Mass Society and Liberal Education," 1954, and "The Structure and Power in American Society," 1958, *Power, Politics & People, The Collected Essays of C. Wright Mills*, edited by Irving Louis Horowitz, Oxford University Press, 1963.

Charter Revision Commission, Fritz Schwartz, and signaled her basic support for their recommendations. The result was that some progressives lined up with Ruth Messinger, while others, including myself, lined up on the side of the opposition (those named above, along with Freddy Ferrer and Ed Rogowsky). Most progressives, however, instead of choosing one side or the other, just dropped the issue.

In November, 1989, the charter revision passed after a lengthy and exhaustive public process. And what were the gains that the Citizens for Charter Change advocates for charter revision won? Here are the three main "victories:"

1. The charter was amended to provide that every Community District shall have a "planner" on staff.
2. The charter was amended to provide that community plans that were authorized under the charter but never implemented for lack of environmental impact studies (costing in the hundreds of thousands of dollars), would have their environmental impact studies paid for by the city.
3. The charter was amended to provide for more strict oversight of quasi-government entities that often pre-empt local review and approvals.

On its face, it sounds pretty good, right? But let's see what really happened after the Charter was revised.

1. Shortly after adoption, community boards asked about their "planners." They were told that they had always had the authority to hire planners, and if they wanted to hire planners they could go right ahead, *within their current budgets* – meaning that they would have to fire their Assistant District Manager or another current employee in order to hire a planner.
2. Before the 1989 charter revision, local community boards were authorized to create their own plans for official adoption by the city. But up until the time of the revision, none were ever heard because the city always bounced the proposed plans back to the local sponsors, demanding that they perform Environmental Impact Statements (EISs) prior to certifying the plans for

public review. An EIS goes beyond environmental issues as the term is generally understood. "Impact" concerns congestion, quality of life, economic and other issues along with pollution, impact on storm drainage and sewer systems, and effect upon wildlife. As an EIS is very costly, none were ever done. After the charter revision, community boards began to prepare new plans for review. But the Department of City Planning *still* would not do any environmental reviews. The city took a new position regarding such plans. They decided that the plans would not require an EIS because they were nothing more than advisory, had no "impact," and therefore would not require an environmental impact statement. The situation went from "plans mean something, but we will not consider them without understanding the impact they will have," to "plans mean nothing so there is no impact." Some victory for the community boards.

3. Another "victory" was the increased control the charter gave the city over quasi-government corporations. These corporations were created with special powers that allowed them to avoid the usual local review requirements for new projects. Local residents and small businesses would often oppose such projects and have an opportunity to challenge them through the usual land use review processes. But with certain "sensitive" projects, instead of going through the usual political process, developable land would be transferred to these entities and the review process would be circumvented. This Charter provision was intended to force all projects to go through conventional public review. After the charter revision passed, the Corporation Counsel for the city of New York simply took the position that the Charter provision was illegal on "pre-emption" grounds. Since these corporations were organized pursuant to state law, the Corporation Counsel decided that state law pre-empts the city's ability to regulate them.

When our progressive group of gadflies lost the battle over the charter revision, we moved on to fight over rulemaking – essentially the rules by which the provisions of the charter would be implemented. These rules, concerning facilities siting and the like, are very important for localities. We were exhaustive in our approach, entirely re-writing the rules for siting incinerators, jails, shelters, waste transfer stations, police academies, and the like. We did this based upon the urging of one member of the City Planning Commission, Jacob Ward, from the Bronx. I would say without hesitation that this Commissioner only made the suggestion to put us off, probably believing that we would never undertake such an effort. He never even read the proposed rules drafted by our group.

By the end of the rulemaking process, we got some beneficial provisions added here and there, but in the end (meaning as these rules are implemented and then quietly amended over time) I'm not sure if all of our hard work really made a difference.

Charter revision is as political a process as there is and is used here as an example of what happens when citizens try to have a political impact. Our group of advocates represented the interests of very substantial portions of the New York City population. We got to contribute to the reams of documents comprising the public record for Charter Revision. But we had no political power so we could pose no real threat. We were merely a few vocal agitators creating a temporary annoyance. In the end, the Charter that was approved was that which was envisioned by those making up the Charter Revision Commission. Once again, the city's major business and real estate interests were victorious.

VIII Culture and Multi-Culturalism

In community development, much is made of the need to preserve, respect, and advance culture, as well as to promote "multi-cultural" development. This requires more than just a simple respect for others; it also mandates a clear sense of our own cultural shortcomings and insensitivities.

When I first began to work as a volunteer with the Northwest Bronx Community and Clergy Coalition, I was young and naïve. At the same time, I was very sure about myself and the world around me. I remember at one meeting a woman reminisced about the "old days" when she and her neighbors could stay outside at all hours of the night and feel safe. But now they no longer felt that way. Now they were surrounded by unfamiliar people who seemed threatening. She complained that the new arrivals made a habit of staying outside at all hours of the night. I had to smile. It seemed she didn't realize she had just told us she herself had done the very same thing when she was young!

I regarded her lack of empathy for the newcomers as stemming from racism. My own sense of culture and the role that it played in community development work was hardly developed at all. This explains why I drew such a simple and wrong-headed conclusion from her remarks. But at the time, similar experiences helped me decide I would be happier working in the South Bronx, where I wouldn't encounter so much "racism."

Centipede Bite. One Saturday in the late seventies, I was on my way to work while my wife and family were still asleep. I lived at 928 Kelly Street and the office was only four doors down the block. As I walked to work, I saw Carol, one of the members of Banana Kelly Community Improvement Association, and we exchanged greetings.

When I arrived at my office, I arranged some papers on my desk, turned on the office's IBM Selectric Typewriter, and went into the bathroom. I was shocked by my image in the mirror. My face was totally swollen.

I ran home and went with my wife to the local hospital where it was determined that the swelling was nothing to worry about. Most likely it was caused by a bite from a centipede. On my arrival back to the block, I once again saw Carol. I asked why she hadn't told me that my face was swollen. With all seriousness, and without a hint of sarcasm or jocularity, she replied, "I thought that's how white people looked when they got up in the morning."

I was reminded of an incident from high school. I was in the boy's locker room and saw a young black student (the only one in the school) entirely naked. I remember thinking to myself, "Damn, even his penis is black." As embarrassing as this is to recall, it serves to illustrate that cultural isolation leads to ignorance, particularly when that isolation is reinforced by the mainstream culture, which in my case meant that white was the norm.

The Norm. I was born in New York City but when I was five years old my parents moved the family out to Long Island. From that point on I grew up in a totally white environment. There was absolutely no racial bigotry in my household. But my surroundings were white and the mainstream media – from magazine articles, to advertisements, to television programs, to commercials, and every other form of media – portrayed white as the norm. Therefore, regardless of the fact that I lived (along with everyone else) in a world comprised of other people, 70% of whom were people of color, in my world white was normal.

What happens when you grow up in a white culture and are not yourself white? I remember my African-American colleague, Carlton Collier, reminiscing about his childhood in Brownsville. He told me that whenever any black person appeared on TV, regardless of the reason, whoever was watching T.V. would yell to everyone else to come quick and see: "There's a colored man on TV!"

Cultural sensitivity is critical to success in urban community development. Yet it is important that we not be ashamed of any culturally determined ignorance we may bring to the table. We should be as tolerant of our own limitations as we would be of others'.

Two Brothers. When I was a young man organizing buildings in the South Bronx I viewed all people living in any particular inner city area as bound to one another in a way that would surely overcome any ethnic prejudice they might have. I, certainly, made no distinction between the various Hispanic populations. I was young, and I considered myself to be a very effective organizer: I had the knack of bringing people together and getting things done. But I remember having an extraordinarily hard time organizing one particular building on Hoe Avenue in the Bronx. This was during the seventies when the South Bronx was losing thousands of units of housing to fires.

The residents of that Hoe Avenue building were all Hispanic. I considered that they were very fortunate to have a hard-working volunteer superintendent who, with his brother, worked tirelessly to maintain the building. This building was one of thousands abandoned by the owner but not yet taken into city ownership through the tax foreclosure process. So I thought the tenants were lucky that someone was keeping the building in good shape.

All the residents seemed to agree that a tenants association would be a good idea. Indeed, I considered it essential for the very survival of the building. Yet somehow this association was never formed. It was a mystery.

I scheduled a tenants meeting for a Saturday afternoon. For one reason or another, the superintendent and his brother were not at the meeting, and for the first time, the residents explained why they had balked about forming a tenants association. They flat-out refused to participate in a tenants association as long as there were "foreigners" in the building.

You may think that they were talking about me – this 23-year old white boy from Long Island who had an answer for every question and an approach to every problem. But no. They were talking about the Mexican brothers who were functioning as volunteer superintendents for the building!

The other tenants were Puerto Ricans. All of the residents were plagued by the same problems: no landlord, sporadic services, and an uncertain future. But the Puerto Ricans refused to work together as long as the Mexicans remained in the building and a part of the group.

This was my first exposure to the negative power of cultural/ethnic bias, and I couldn't do a thing about it.

Finally, Jose Madrigal and his brother moved to another building. Jose eventually became a homesteader in Banana Kelly's first sweat equity project, and he went on to lead a second such project on Fox Street. For a while, he functioned as Banana Kelly's construction manager before starting his own rehab company. I am not sure if the building on Hoe Avenue survived, but Jose became a successful contractor and community leader.

Urban Flux. The beauty and the challenge, the attraction and the frightening reality of New York (like every major international city), is that it is ever in flux, ever changing its face and adjusting its functions. When I began to work in the South Bronx in the early seventies, it was almost entirely inhabited by Puerto Ricans. Over the next twenty years, the number of Puerto Ricans diminished yet the population increased from its low point in the late seventies as Mexicans, Haitians, Jamaicans and Dominicans moved in. In 1974, you could have probably put New York's Dominicans in one small auditorium. Today, New York's Dominican population is over half a million.

Urban change is relentless and necessary to the long-term health and viability of the city. The cultural challenges that accompany change must be accommodated in community development efforts.

Fostering Collaboration. The fact of the matter is that Puerto Ricans (at least among the first and second generations) prefer to live with Puerto Ricans. Dominicans prefer to live with Dominicans. Mexicans prefer to live with Mexicans, just as some of my ancestors – first generation Irish and Italians –

preferred to live with other Irish and Italian families. In my community development work, I have sought to neither promote nor discourage "ethnic clustering." However, I sought to promote development that accommodates all ethnic components of the neighborhood, seeking every opportunity to bring people of different backgrounds together around issues of potential concern, such as education, safe streets, affordable housing, and child care. I provided many opportunities for interaction where collaboration had obvious benefits to different ethnic groups.

To be honest, fostering this sort of collaboration is one of the more difficult aspects of community development. But it is also one of the most satisfying, because of its potential.

Take for example the early development of Banana Kelly. That curved section of Kelly Street, known as Banana Kelly, was an area anomaly: it was mostly made up of African-Americans, perhaps because the landlord with the most occupied buildings on the block, Frank Potts, was himself black. Starting as a superintendent who eventually took ownership of the building he serviced, he purchased one building at a time until he owned seven buildings on that one block.

When I started organizing on Kelly Street, the organization was primarily made up of young African-American members. Soon, however, with Mildred Velez and others on board, Puerto Ricans became part of the leadership group. I believe that my involvement, combined with the extreme circumstances of the time, broke down cultural prejudices that could have gotten in the way of collaboration and ultimate success.

The Character of Culture. What is the "culture" in "multi-culturalism"? Is it the language and traditions associated with a particular country of origin? Is it what people eat and how they build houses as well as the music they play and the poems they write? For me, culture is the expression of people living and working collectively within an environment as they attempt to understand, enjoy, and ultimately transform their shared circumstances. Culture results from the interaction with and transformation of a given environment through shared human endeavor. Although the expression of culture can be personal, its character is always collective. Tools, musical instruments, art, story-telling, religion, work habits, recreational approaches, and humor have all developed through collective deliberation and action. As we form new groups, new cultural expressions will develop. While I value the importance of ethnic cultural heritage, I believe it is possible to complement this with newly emerging cultural expression, and this process can occur across ethnic lines.

For example, go to a tenants' meeting in a building where there are people from different ethnic backgrounds. At the meeting, you will observe nuances that are specific to this group of people and no other. References to past experiences and practices, the manner in which they deal with one another, jokes that resonate with the group but not with you, the outsider – all suggesting that a new cultural dynamic has arisen out of the residents' interactions as they manage their common circumstances: the building, its residents, the bank, the superintendent, the seniors. This same cultural development evolves from every newly initiated set of human interactions for the purpose of transforming common human circumstances. And this does not require that any other cultural character be set-aside or subsumed. The tenants' meeting might end with multi-ethnic refreshments and music – and with cross-cultural sharing. For example, African-Americans may joke around with phrases spoken in Spanish. "Don't believe her. She's a *bochinchera*!" (This means one who gossips.)

American Isolation. Unlike Latino culture, American culture seems to be based on isolation, precisely because our values downplay community and promote the "rugged" individual and the family as the primary social units. But isolation is anathema to culture, as well as to community and democracy. Culture must be nourished through ongoing collective human endeavor in order to survive.

If culture must function within some community setting to thrive, and if multi-culturalism is inevitable, then we have to accept and embrace the potential for a supra-culture – one which develops inter-culturally, superimposing itself as both a bridge between, and a protective shield for, separate ethnic cultures, as in the tenants' meeting example above.

Community developers should seek to respect and preserve ethnic pride, while simultaneously creating new forms of cultural expression arising out of collective endeavor.

VIII Social Capital

The concept of social capital is important in the field of community development. Social capital is something like the concept of "goodwill" in business: it is real and valuable, albeit intangible. Lately, it has gained increasing currency among researchers, commentators and practitioners. Today, social capital is often referred to in grant applications, publications, policy papers, and web pages.

Its origins, however, date back to 1916, when a practical reformer of the Progressive era, L. J. Hanifan, State Supervisor of rural schools in West Virginia, first used the term. His definition entailed such intangibles as goodwill, fellowship, sympathy, and social intercourse.[47]

Some Recent Definitions of Social Capital. A more recent definition posits that social capital refers to

> those stocks of social trust, norms and networks that people can draw upon to solve common problems. Networks of civic engagement, such as neighborhood associations, sports clubs, and cooperatives are an essential form of social capital, and the denser the networks, the more likely that members of a community will cooperate for mutual benefit.[48]

---

[47] Robert D. Putnam, *Bowling Alone*, Simon & Schuster, 2000, p.19.
[48] University of Washington at www.gspa.washington.edu/trust/links/capital.html/

By "denser," the writer means a large of bank of varied resources: contacts with educators, police officials, government officials, religious leaders, professionals, and the media.

The World Bank's website defines social capital as

> the institutions, relationships, and norms that shape the quality and quantity of society's interactions.

These are "critical for societies to prosper economically." Social capital is

> not just the sum of the institutions which underpin a society – it is the glue that holds them together.[49]

It is interesting that in the World Bank information on social capital, substantial emphasis is placed on its downside. Specifically, the website refers to the "problem" of closed communities using their close-knit connectedness and social capital to prevent "progress" by refusing interaction outside of their community, tribe, clan or other social unit. But the World Bank probably would object to any monetary system that is not denominated in the currency acceptable to World Bank and easily accessible for government taxation and subsequent debt payment: that is, the U.S. dollar.

Thomas Ford Brown writes that

> social capital is a processual system for allocating resources across a social network according to a pattern of relations among the individual egos that comprise that network.[50]

He quotes Alejandro Portes, who has written that social capital is

---

[49] World Bank Web Site at www.worldbank.org/poverty/scapital/whatsc.html
[50] Thomas Ford Brown, Theoretical Perspectives on Social Capital, at http://jhunx.hcf.jhu.edu/tombrown/econsoc/soccap.html

the capacity of individuals to command scarce resources by virtue of their membership in networks or broader social structures.... The ability to obtain [social capital] does not inhere in the individual... but instead is a property of the individual's set of relationships with others. Social capital is the product of embeddedness.[51]

Community and Social Capital. In the literature, there is little about how social capital is related to community. However, it should be clear from the definitions above that there is at least some relationship between social capital and community. I maintain that social capital is the currency of community and that without community there is no social capital. When Alejandro Portes writes that social capital is the "product of embeddedness," there has got to be a context for that embeddedness. That context is community.

Understanding Social Capital. The importance of social capital is best conveyed through an analogy. I mentioned earlier that social capital is the currency of community. Let us examine how money – our currency – operates in a closed community.

First, we must understand the true nature of money by removing its mystique. Money has three basic attributes. It is a medium of exchange, an IOU, and a store of value. All three attributes are important to an understanding of how money (and, by analogy, social capital) works.

That money is a medium of exchange is its most obvious attribute for most of us. Go anywhere in the United States (and much of the world) and the U.S. dollar is accepted as a medium of exchange for goods and services.

The second attribute of money is that it is an IOU. This is a bit more difficult to understand. A dollar bill theoretically indicates that some value has been produced within the economic system by the holder of that dollar bill, and upon presentation of this bill for payment, the IOU is being called.

---

[51] Alejandro Portes, *The Economic Sociology and the Sociology of Immigration: A Conceptual Overview*, as found in Thomas Ford Brown article, *ibid.*

Lets say that there are four people in a closed economy. Bill makes shoes for Mary. Mary gives Bill an IOU for the shoes. Bill now has a piece of paper that is, for all practical purposes, money. In a closed community or economic system, Bill can now go to anyone else in that system or community and exchange that IOU for something of like value. So Bill goes to Hector and receives some home improvement work in return for Mary's IOU. Hector goes to Jaqueline and secures some service, again in return for Mary's IOU. Eventually, the IOU goes back to Mary and she has to make good on her promise to deliver a good or service of equivalent value for the shoes that she initially received from Bill. Perhaps she will bake some pies for Jacqueline.

A number of points are worth mentioning here. First, the IOU is money. Second, in return for the shoes she received, Mary does not have a specific obligation to Bill. Rather, she has an obligation to the community of persons that comprise the economic system within which the IOU (currency) operates. This sense of "generalized reciprocity" is important to the concept of community, as well as to the currency of community, social capital.

Finally, the IOU is functioning as a "store of value," money's third attribute. Take note that in the transactions elaborated on above there is no interest that accrues to the holder of Mary's IOU. That is because there is balance in the system, and at the time the IOU is called, the value of the returned service or good is equivalent in then-current terms to the original pair of shoes that Mary received. Now, if Mary abuses her position in the community, her currency, her IOU, her social capital in the community will depreciate until it becomes worthless or she works extra hard to make up for overextending her social capital.

Social capital is the currency of community. And just like currency, it allows community members to call on collectively available resources for personal use. This currency is normative, as opposed to being tangible (i.e. "hard currency"). And it is what makes community work. In *Bowling Alone*,[52] Putnam refers to numerous research projects that directly connect social capital to

---

[52] Putnam, R. Op. cit., p.290.

child welfare and education, healthy and productive neighborhoods, economic prosperity, health, happiness, and functioning democracy.

Social Capital and Helping Activities. In the field of community development in this country, social capital is most often manifested in what Professor Susan Saegert of CUNY Graduate Center refers to as "helping" activities.[53] An older neighbor may watch the baby of a single-mom needing to go to work. A younger resident with a car may shop for a home-bound resident. A neighbor may agree to coach a sports team. These helping activities can create the benefits to which Putnam refers. For instance, elder members watching the children of other members may provide the side benefit of providing homework help for the children they watch, and leaving children with a caring elder allows the younger members to pursue employment opportunities, further benefiting their children's welfare.

In these cases, there is some semblance of community. There is, of course, the commonality that comes from residing at the same address. There is interdependence, since those making up the community (it need not include all the residents in the building) are reliant on one another for necessities and to enhance quality of life. And there is collective capacity, at least in one very real sense. By helping one another, whether by improving the quality of life or allowing for individuals to go out and work, they collectively increase their ability to continue residing in that building .

Once we get beyond the building, however, finding community is more difficult. In the inner city, helping activities are often constrained by oppressive local circumstances.

When I was an organizer in the 1970s, organizing was not as difficult as it is now. At that time, there were social networks that extended throughout a

---

[53] This concept is found in most of Dr. Saegert's publications. "Helping activities" as an incident of social health within a building and neighborhood context is a theme that runs throughout her work. Examples are: Susan Saegert, *Social Capital and Poor Communities*, Russell Sage Foundation Publications, 2001; Jacqueline Leavitt and Susan Saegert, *From Abandonment to Hope: Community Households in Harlem,* Columbia University Press, 1990.

neighborhood that could be tapped into for some defined organizing purpose. Even in the most severely distressed neighborhoods, such as the South Bronx, each block had social networks, social capital, and some semblance of an established community – even if only in a defensive sense (the power to be safe, to exclude anti-social elements, to stop crime).

So when I began organizing on Kelly Street in the seventies, there were informal social networks that prevented isolation and vulnerability and also allowed for the flow of important information: the opening of a new senior or day care center, imminent school or firehouse closings, ways to deal with particular teachers, the best place to find good produce, what to do to prevent an unwarranted eviction, how to help plan a block party.

This redeeming dynamic was devastated in large part by the fires that ravaged inner city neighborhoods in the 1970s and the crack epidemic that ravaged an entire generation of young people in the late 1980s and early 1990s. The social networks that permeated blocks have been largely destroyed. Social capital has been depleted. Community has been lost. People feel unsafe even in the lobbies of their buildings. Neighbors do not trust each other. One will say, "I will not attend a meeting that *her* son may be at."

In organizing buildings today, it is a delicate matter just to decide in whose apartment the initial meeting will take place. Only certain people are trusted, and these people must become the nexus for the new organizing project.

When illegal activity subsides, as occurred in the 1990's, people do emerge from their homes and begin to re-establish social contacts. But this is a return to neighborliness, not really a re-building of community. The rebuilding of community and the re-establishment of social capital will take much longer to recreate than it took to destroy. That is because social capital is the currency of community, so social capital cannot be re-introduced without the rebuilding of community. In many areas, once community is destroyed, absent a radical reformation of economic, social, and political forces, the question is whether or not it can ever be rebuilt, even with the help of the most effective organizers.

The Concept of Community

IX Community Organizing

Saul Alinsky is the father of modern-day community organizing, and successive generations of organizers owe their perspectives and techniques to this giant. Some of the most successful groups in the country, including ACORN, Industrial Areas Foundation (IAF), and National Peoples Action, are among the heirs of the Alinsky tradition. To this day, Alinsky's book, *Rules for Radicals*, remains a mainstay for young organizers.

Harry C. Boyte contends that there are three elements to Alinsky's approach:

1. organizing people for power;
2. building indigenous leadership to take charge of the organizations created;
3. organizing to win.

Boyte notes that

> Alinsky was extraordinarily creative... He believed in using tactics within the constituency's range of experience [and] he urged tactics full of surprises, irreverence, drama and rapid change...[54]

---

[54] Harry C. Boyte, *The Backyard Revolution*, Temple University Press, 1980, pp50-51.

In later years, Alinsky moved from a focus on the have-nots to strategies that were more inclusive of the middle class.

Who Really Leads? I have worked with many organizing groups, and over the years I have noticed that many leaders never want to give up control to developing indigenous leadership. This violates Alinsky's second element: developing the capacity locally to exist without the organizer.[55]

Betraying these underlying principles of organizing can lead to perverse results. I once had the opportunity to work with a group of parents who were upset because a local IAF group had organized them to vote for a parents association for their school. However, when the "wrong" people were elected by the parents, the organizers went to the school superintendent and convinced him to nullify the election on the grounds that more IAF "training" was needed. One parent even complained to me that those parents in opposition to the IAF organizers were sometimes invited to meetings in the wrong locations or at the wrong times to ensure they did not attend. Here's where creative organizing shades into dirty tricks.

As an amusing aside, Alinsky was not above a little chicanery when it was absolutely necessary. During the Depression, Alinsky (like many others) was unemployed and often hungry. He developed a technique whereby he would go to a chain cafeteria and order a cup of coffee. When he got the check for five cents, he would pocket the check, claim that he lost it, obtain another one to pay with, and then leave. He would then go to another cafeteria in the chain, order a steak dinner, pocket that check, pull out the bill for the coffee, and pay five cents for the steak dinner. He then told other hungry workers and college students to follow the same procedure:

---

[55] In this regard, ACORN departs from the Alinsky ideal: rather, it follows the labor model of organization – a strong central organization, with dependent, responsive, local chapters. The National People's Action, a Chicago-based group, is the best example of an organization that adheres to Alinsky principles. It remains to be seen if that continues with the loss of its dynamic leader, Gail Cincotta.

I stood on the lectern and explained my system in detail, with the help of a big map of Chicago with all the local branches of the cafeteria marked on it. Social ecology! I split my recruits up into squads according to territory; one team would work the South Side for lunch, another the North Side for dinner, and so on. We got the system down to a science, and for six months all of us were eating free. Then the bastards brought in those serial machines at the door where you pull out a ticket that's only good for that particular cafeteria. That was a low blow. We were the first victims of automation.[56]

Ongoing Organizing. For groups like ACORN and IAF, it sometimes seems that the organizing never stops. These groups are apparently compelled to organize one campaign after another to keep their membership engaged and active. In their article, "Community Organizing and Comprehensive Community Initiatives," Mark Joseph and Renee Ogletree write:

Community organizing ...[is] an ongoing process rather than merely a phase or outreach strategy of a community-building effort.[57]

But organizing is *not* an ongoing process, at least with respect to any particular community. However, it is *seen* as a never-ending process to many organizing groups – precisely because of the absence of community! In the place of true community, there must be a mechanism (ongoing organizing) to incessantly create a convening dynamic for the community. When this convening dynamic does not occur through everyday life, then there is a need to organize constantly.

Any formulation that sees organizing as an ongoing process views the local institution as a service provider to the residents of an area, and not as a servant to the people. In defining community organizing as an ongoing process, the very concept of community is placed on its head. Instead of community institutions being the vehicles for accomplishing the common goals and sought-after outcomes of community, the "community institution" takes the place of community by setting the rules of engagement and the processes for participation.

---

[56] *Playboy* magazine, March 1972, p.64.
[57] Stone, R. Op. cit., pp. 94-95.

So the community institution becomes an institutionalized surrogate community. Once this happens, all efforts maintain the sponsoring institution at the center of every initiative.

I believe that organizing, like leadership, is *not* a permanent condition. The permanent condition is the changed social, economic and political structures that permit the ongoing process of democracy to occur on a local level. In this way, mobilization can occur around issues as needed. Once the agenda is set and the capacity developed or obtained, the organizing stops. What doesn't stop is the constant interaction of community participants in their social, economic, and political activities, and the coming and going of leaders who emerge to take on an issue and then go back to their lives. Interaction is constant, education is ongoing, and the relationships are defined by the structures and processes of community, *not the structures of an organizing agenda.*[58]

The Pathology of Poverty. Today, there is a disturbing view within the field that regards poverty as a pathology. This is evident from the terms used to describe certain organizing techniques: values clarification, self-esteem training, and health realization. These terms start from the premise that people need to be taught morals and values; that people must be given knowledge; that they can be taught to be empowered and taught to trust. There is little respect for people's individuality or their life experiences. To paraphrase Paulo Freire, people are treated as vessels that must be purged of the wrong kind of experiences, values, and perspectives, and then filled with the right ones.

Mobilization. Mobilization efforts in organizing are issue-specific. People are mobilized around an issue of concern. It is an approach that is most Alinsky-like and is employed very effectively by national organizing groups as well as many successful local organizing groups. However, as a comprehensive organizing approach, it is lacking. There is little in the way of long-term planning or deliberations regarding comprehensive structural change. The energy of the

---

[58] I make this argument in Chapin Hall, *ibid*, p. 98.

initiative expires with the resolution of the issue. That is why groups like ACORN seem to be constantly bouncing from one campaign to another. Stringing together issues/victories through successive campaigns is necessary to maintain their membership, sustain their leadership, and demonstrate their power to those of influence on the outside. The theory is that it is absolutely necessary to produce results to keep people involved. As stated by Ron Shiffman,

> It does represent success, and, as Alinsky stated, picking winnable wars is the first step toward transformation.[59]

Toward Transformation. But there are many who disagree. The first step towards "transformation" is not choosing winnable wars, but rather attaining a critical understanding of the source of the problem. This is a difficult first step, which is probably why so many in the advocacy community feel compelled to deliver a tangible result instead.

The ability to assess our political, social and economic circumstances is the first step towards transformation because it results in a redefinition of ourselves in relation to the rest of the world. "They" often seem to be in control of our lives and circumstances, and proper understanding helps demystify "them" and suggests possible solutions to our problems. The second step towards transformation is to talk to others in the "same boat" and help them discover viable explanations and devise effective actions. The third step towards transformation is the joining of "word and deed," which is the beginning of power. Although this power can be exercised ad hoc and targeted to a specific purpose (through mobilization), most often this power is manifested through more substantive developmental organizing.

Developmental Organizing. Developmental organizing takes place to address an issue of common concern with the understanding that the concern is basic enough to require sustained organizational attention. The job of the organizer is

---

[59] Shiffman, R. Op. cit., p. 28.

to develop the organizational (institutional) capacity to address that issue in the long term. This new institution (or newly transformed institution) is then the vehicle by which the community implements its agenda regarding that issue and the vehicle by which the community interacts with others in the larger society.

Developmental organizing is difficult. It requires patience and a subrogation of ego on the part of the organizer, for the organizer has a role that may require him or her to step into the background – or to step aside entirely. In the organizing field, it is relatively easy to mobilize against a recognizable enemy or an obvious injustice. It is much more difficult to organize ("develop") the institutional capacity to address issues of common concern over the long term, and to alter the power-relationships that fostered basic injustice to begin with. If the organizer makes the mistake of "developing leadership" before developing the organization, all he or she will have accomplished will be to replace an outside demagogue with an inside demagogue.

I have dealt with many such demagogues in my thirty years of working in this field. One such "leader" from the Oceanhill-Brownsville section of Brooklyn often took to railing against whites who would dare to come into his area and start a development program, raising funds and earning fees in the process. His position was that if anyone was going to treat his mostly African-American neighborhood like a plantation and its people like slaves, it would be him.

In my outreach to the residents of Melrose Commons, I saw a process that was "déjà vu all over again." As mentioned earlier, the reformed planning initiative began with a forum at Lincoln Hospital, where residents, led by local leader Pedro Cintron, charged Bronx Center leaders with conspiring to destroy their homes and their neighborhoods.

After that Saturday morning forum, we began to have regular Tuesday "informational sessions" at a local church. By the second or third such meeting, Cintron and other local leaders quietly but forcefully took the control of the meeting from me. My allowing that transfer of control was important to the eventual success of the initiative. From that point on, the agenda became their agenda. The Borough President, Fernando Ferrer, ensured the presence of key government officials at these meetings, and it soon became clear that the local agenda would prevail. The Tuesday forums were supplemented by a planning studio that transformed the urban renewal program block-by-block from a plan that displaced and entirely rebuilt the area, to one that provided for minimal displacement and required redevelopment that integrated the old with the new.

So far, so good. There was the semblance of community that had not been recognized by outsiders, including myself. Local residents trusted one another. The leadership was responsive to the concerns of residents. They developed their own institution called, the Nos Quedamos/We Stay Committee to implement the agenda that was defined by the residents themselves. And decision-making was inclusive and deliberative.

But after several months, as the initiative was becoming more successful, Pedro Cintron died. His leadership position was assumed by Yolanda Garcia, who owned a business in the area. Yolanda had been active with the group from the very beginning, but worked mostly in the background. With Pedro's demise, she was the logical person to step forward and lead the effort. Ultimately, she proved herself to be more charismatic than Pedro and very capable. She was intelligent, had the ability to devote time to the effort and she worked hard at making it successful. But as she made more contacts and learned the field, she began to distance herself from the organization's members. She would highlight differences between leaders and then place herself in the middle to reconcile those differences. She took information and contacts, and once she made them her own, she would marginalize those who had first brought them to her. She ingratiated herself to certain politicians and represented herself as central to the group's success. In the process, the group quickly evolved into a typical CDC – one that was funded to deliver services and in which the leader was eventually more accountable to outside funding sources than to resident members.

By most measures, the group is a success. The urban renewal plan is being implemented, albeit slowly and in phases. The group has a good reputation with funders and government. Unfortunately, Yolanda Garcia recently passed away, but not before establishing a capable and productive CDC. Her daughter took over the reins of the organization without any real preparation or training.

But by all outward appearances, she is doing a commendable job of continuing her mother's legacy in the implementation of the Melrose Commons Urban Renewal Plan. However, as a community-building effort, which it initially had the potential of becoming, Nos Quedamos failed. It reminded me of the work I had done at Banana Kelly in the mid-seventies when the exact same process occurred: as funding came in and the demands of "professionalism" increased, its leaders became its managers, its organizers became its employees, and its members became its clients. In talking to Ron Shiffman, I likened the Banana Kelly transformation to the Nos Quedamos change. He replied that perhaps this is the natural way for such initiatives to progress. I think he is wrong. I think we can work for more positive outcomes.

Private Troubles/Public Issues. In his 1959 essay, C. Wright Mills makes a useful distinction between "private troubles" and "public issues."[60]

> Troubles have to do with an individual's character and with those limited areas of social life of which he is directly and personally aware... issues have to do with matters that transcend these local environments of the individual and the limited range of his life... An issue is a public matter.

We are all confronted with "troubles" at one time or another. The problem is that as we become more isolated socially and as our connection to others becomes more remote, more of what once would be construed as "public issues" become instead "private troubles." For example, if there is a functioning local economy and a family bread-winner is injured or killed, the other members of that community feel the loss and have a vested interest in helping that family survive. So temporarily assisting the family and then helping them to maintain a business or gain productive employment is seen as a "public issue." But with individual/household isolation and the concomitant loss of community, the equivalent event is a now undeniably a "private trouble."

---

[60] C. Wright Mills, *Power, Politics & People,* The Collected Essays of C. Wright Mills, Ed. Irving Louis Horowitz, *The Big City: Private Troubles and Public Issues,* Op. cit., p.395.

When can a private trouble be made into a public issue? It can be done when the private trouble has relevance to sufficient numbers of people who are somehow connected to one another and can share their experiences. The first barrier to overcome is the isolation felt by those individuals confronted by similar troubles. The second barrier is that set of public sentiments that establishes the values of the majority. When there is a push to advance a social agenda, much public debate revolves around the values we are trying to protect and encourage. For example, if we focus on personal responsibility as a primary value – the very same value extolled in the welfare reform debate of the mid-nineties – then what we are really doing is making a public judgment that the problem of poverty is personal and so we need to frame our public policies to accommodate personal weaknesses and failings ("private troubles"). Conversely, we are assuming that the current economic, political and social systems advance the general welfare for all but those whose failings create self-imposed obstacles to personal progress.

If, on the other hand, the values we sought to promote were every individual's right to employment as well as the right to attain a certain minimum standard of living through higher minimum wages, guaranteed health care, and the like, then the public judgment would ultimately result in more progressive policies and the transfers of wealth dedicated to those goals.

If our accepted public judgment was based upon the right to full employment and livable wages for all who work, we wouldn't have a system where some people work two or three jobs and still can't afford health care while others earn hundreds of millions of dollars a year. In a single year, 2006, hedge fund manager James Simons earned $1.7 billion.[61]

Organizing is Political. All organizing that seeks any redress is necessarily going against the prevailing political order. That is why all developmental organizing is necessarily and ultimately political. Developmental organizing is about changing the structure and balance of power-sharing arrangements. This

---

[61] Paul Krugman, "Gilded Once More," *The New York Times*, April 27, 2007.

is in contrast to issues-organizing that seeks redress from those in power only for a particular issue. Once those in power address the issue, everyone goes home and the matter is closed, and there is no change in power sharing arrangements. In fact, when convenient (and that is most of the time), those in power are free to take away that which they have given, a trend that began in the Reagan administration and continues to this day.

Developmental organizing is painstaking, frustrating, and time-consuming, but it is the only way to organize for the long term. Only by organizing developmentally can we hope to make such an impact on existing political, social, and economic structures, systems and processes.

Providing a Map. About midway through his excellent book, *The Tipping Point*,[62] Malcolm Gladwell relates a story about a Yale University professor, Howard Leventhal, who wanted to see if he could persuade college students to obtain inoculations. He used different motivational tactics, ranging from the coolly educational to the downright scary. Still, only about 3% of the students actually obtained a shot (even though students exposed to the scarier tactics initially appeared to be very convinced about the necessity for inoculation).

Then the professor repeated the experiment – with one small change. This time, he provided the students with a campus map, with the health clinic clearly marked, along with the clinic's hours of operation. The inoculation rate jumped from 3% to 23%, with those who got shots evenly divided among the different motivational groups. The professor ultimately concluded that:

> Students needed to know how to fit the tetanus stuff into their lives; the addition of the map and the times... shifted the booklet from an abstract lesson in medical risk – a lesson no different from the countless other academic lessons they had received over their academic career – to a practical and personal piece of medical advice. And once the advice became practical and personal, it became memorable.[63]

---

[62] Malcolm Gladwell, *The Tipping Point*, Little Brown, 2000.
[63] *Ibid*, p.98.

Many more students acted upon that advice once they had the map – even though most of them already knew the location of the clinic!

From the Abstract to the Personal. The challenge of organizing is to go from the abstract to the personal: to frame a message, define an issue, and encourage a course of action in ways that break through theoretical notions of justice and relate directly to the everyday lives of the people. If it does not fit into the everyday lives of people, if it is not "practical and personal," then organizing will not be effective. I cannot stress this point enough.

Let me return to an experience I mentioned in Chapter 1. I was working in a building on Villa Avenue which had no hot water, only sporadic heat, and no functioning front door lock. To me, these problems were obvious organizing fodder, and I could not understand why no matter how hard I tried, the residents resisted me. One day a kindly, older gentleman approached me and said, "Son, you are wasting your time. Do you have any idea how much I pay for rent? Exactly $67 a month. I am not all that happy with some of the problems in the building but I am very happy that my rent is low and affordable. So do yourself a favor. Leave the people in this building alone. We have no interest in what you are doing."

I was not connecting to the real concerns of those particular residents. Instead of being seen as a help, I was viewed as a terrible threat.

When I started organizing on Kelly Street, I had much more success. On Kelly Street, in contrast to the surrounding blocks, there was a core group of residents who wanted to remain living right where they were. So my talks about self-help, sweat equity and local economic development fit right into their lives.

The "After-Meeting." About ten years later I became involved in a planning project called "Bronx Center," which had an organizing component we came to call the "Bronx Community Forum." Contrary to my approach at Banana Kelly, I had no intention of moving into the neighborhood to better identify with the residents and help lead from within. So, to my way of thinking, my job was to provide information that residents claimed was not forthcoming, to provide access to decision-makers, and (most importantly) to facilitate the use of public space for residents to publicly respond to what they heard and to dialogue with their neighbors.

At the Melrose Commons meetings, plenty of time was provided for public-hearing types of exchanges and also for cross-dialogue among residents (the GEM or Group Enhancement Model). Even if the formal agenda required a presentation and "bi-lateral" back and forth comments, no meeting ever ended until the informal "after-meeting" was done. The "after-meeting" is that part of the meeting when the formal meeting is ended and the people stay around, socialize and discuss among themselves the event, the information shared, and plans for acting on that information. In any community organizing effort, this is the most important part of the meeting.

But the Melrose residents took this even farther. Unbeknownst to me or the other organizers, between our regular Tuesday evening forums a series of other meetings was taking place, and at these meetings they decided to take over the entire organizing effort. So at one Tuesday night forum about three or four weeks into the process, I was politely asked to cede the facilitating to the newly formed Nos Quedamos/We Stay Committee, which I was proud and delighted to do. Then this committee began holding planning forums during which the residents, with the help of a volunteer planner and architect, Petr Stand, completely re-designed the urban renewal plan, block-by-block.

Two Ways of Looking at a Story. Soon after, I attended a forum sponsored by the federal Department of Housing and Urban Development (HUD), and I proudly told this story to a group of government bureaucrats and community leaders from other parts of the country. I regarded the incident as a success in local organizing, so I was perplexed when an HUD official said that he was very sorry that all of my hard work had been in vain. After that, others began commiserating with me over my assumed failure to retain control of the situation.

To me, the real point of the story was that this initial organizing effort was a tremendous success! The bureaucrats' sympathy betrayed an attitude that is unfortunately pervasive in the public and private service sectors: i.e., that poor people are unable to manage their own lives and that professionals are needed to teach, to guide, to discipline (when necessary) and generally to supervise them in their daily pursuits. It is, of course, an attitude that is anathema to any true organizing approach.

The urban renewal plan was a real and tangible threat to residents and local business people alike. The message and the method (regular Tuesday evening forums at a local church and the early supplemental meetings at a storefront at the home of one of the local leaders) "fit" well into people's lives. A project that called for 100% displacement was certainly "personal." And by providing outside (and appropriate) technical assistance, the effort was practical.

As a practical step, the first action I took was to hire an organizer, Sandra Colon, and place her at the disposal of the residents. She proved to be an excellent organizer and taught me much in the years we worked together. She continued to work with the residents after the Nos Quedamos group seized control. There were other reasons that the group was successful. The Bronx Borough President, Fernando Ferrer, placed the resources of his office at the disposal of the resident committee and made his staff accessible and accountable. He also made the Mayor's (Dinkins) approval of the revised plan one of the conditions of his support for Dinkins' reelection bid. Richard Kahan, a man of immense government and private sector influence, pulled in technical advisors of all kinds to assist the planning effort. Melrose Commons became a success in a very short period of time. And Ron Shiffman, even though needing to remain in the background because of his position on the City Planning Commission, was able, with the consent of the Chair of the Commission, to provide some guidance to the effort until Giuliani became Mayor.

CATCH. I had – and retained – a more direct role in is the development of a citywide mutual housing association called Community Assisted Tenant Controlled Housing (CATCH). CATCH is organized under a "mother-daughter" mutual housing model: there is an umbrella organization that mobilizes resources, staffs the local and citywide operations, provides back office support, and generally directs citywide efforts (advocacy, funding, broad-based policy). Under this umbrella are numerous smaller, local mutual housing associations. CATCH was developed to provide a mechanism for resident control of housing by low and moderate income families without their having to purchase cooperative shares and provide for their own staffing and property management services.

The organizing technique we utilized at CATCH was developmental organizing. It was organizing that develops organizations: local, resident-controlled, democratic institutions that can provide services to its members. Since CATCH targets distressed real estate, our work was initially straightforward. After the hard work of eliminating drug and other illegal activity in the buildings, our organizing revolved around the need for repairs and renovation.

During this initial organizing stage the primary concerns of residents concerned relocation during the renovation and rent levels once renovation was completed. In most cases, we were able to convince residents that the process was difficult but manageable and that they would all be able to continue to live in their buildings at affordable rents. From there, we usually sought to involve the residents in some aspects of design, renovation and temporary relocation. This involvement was sustained through the renovation process. So far, so good.

The Long Term. The challenge of developmental organizing is to sustain interest and substantive participation over the long term and to use the resident-controlled institution as a vehicle for changing the dynamics of local and citywide power-sharing arrangements.

CATCH has organized active membership committees and solid leadership during the physical redevelopment phase of each project. But having grown from 70 units in two neighborhoods in 1994 to over 800 units in six neighborhoods by 2007, CATCH has become too big to be personal as a single convening entity. So CATCH has employed a number of techniques in an attempt to ensure the long-term viability of its local mutual housing associations (MHAs). CATCH itself is a citywide MHA.

For the second time in ten years the organization is conducting a resident asset survey. Through such a survey it is hoped that issues of concern to residents will come to the surface. More importantly, CATCH hopes to find out about the hidden resources within its membership base. When the first survey was completed, CATCH learned of religious and civic affiliations, as well as talents and skills that the organization was able to use to help its local MHAs and earn extra income for the members. For instance, upon finding out that many of CATCH's members cleaned houses and offices as a way of earning money, CATCH initiated its own cleaning company. Upon learning that Ida Bibbs was an expert seamstress, we found her work through the Parodneck Foundation. Residents with valuable professional experience, teachers, police officers, health professionals, and others, were tapped as needed for special projects.

In community organizing, social events are very important. It is through socializing and planning social events that strong bonds are formed. CATCH is planning to have more social activities: picnics, parties, dances. CATCH also recognizes the importance of regular communications between board members, staff, and the community. So it publishes regular newsletters. This helps people appreciate their organization. Once they see how the local Central Harlem MHA, the South Bronx MHA and so on benefit their neighborhoods and the city as a whole, they are likely to have a greater allegiance to CATCH. People like to read about what they are a part of, and they like to contribute to publications and see their names in print. CATCH is using social events and newsletters to engage and capture an active resident base in the hopes of building an economically-viable, politically-relevant, and powerful system of local, resident-controlled institutions as part of a citywide mutual housing network.

Nonetheless, with all its potential, it remains to be seen if CATCH can develop into a truly sustainable organization through its developmental organizing technique, or whether the group will eventually grow content with merely being a competent community development corporation. In the Central Harlem and Washington Heights MHAs – those local affiliated MHAs that are most advanced – residents and leaders are beginning to make important connections between resident engagement, participation, and the bottom line of the housing entities.

What exactly does this mean? Low and moderate income housing is difficult to manage and maintain. Many not-for-profit sponsors develop projects with studios and 1-bedroom apartments. They do this for three reasons:

1. development fees are calculated by the unit;
2. once a project contains three bedrooms, there is a requirement for one and one-half bathrooms, thus increasing cost, but mostly:
3. small units are ultimately occupied by seniors and young professionals, making them much easier and cheaper to maintain.

CATCH's properties are developed for families with children (including teens), which is challenging.

So there is a direct connection between the ability of low income family housing to survive financially and the manner in which the residents themselves treat and protect this affordable housing resource. If the families do not control their children; if rent is not paid; if residents do not participate in community events; if residents do not take on a proprietary attitude, the bottom lines of the projects suffer and ultimately fail.

Beyond this "survival recognition," CATCH members are beginning to recognize the potential that a true community organization can realize: economically (with its purchasing power, including spending its dollars locally), socially (the ability to amass, build and utilize social capital), and politically (the ability to collectively make demands on public resources on an equal footing with others operating in the public sector).

To the organizers of today, I extend my deepest respect and admiration. Organizing is difficult work, work in which personal gratification often comes from factoring the organizer out of the equation. Today, those taking up the mantle do not have the opportunities of past organizers to tap into formal and informal social networks that greatly expedite legitimization, communication and mobilization. But as hard as the work it is, it is also indispensable to community-building and to efforts that join people in working for meaningful change.

X Bias, Prejudice, and Racism

At dinner, a good friend and colleague once paid me what he considered the ultimate compliment. He said that I was color-blind. I told him I did not view it as a compliment at all. Rather, I saw it as an indictment.

This led to a prolonged discussion of three related concepts: bias, prejudice and racism and how one is distinguished from the other. We agreed that these elements are lurking just below the surface of almost every community effort, ready to emerge in one form or another.

Bias. Bias that is based purely on ignorance is relatively easy to overcome. Bias results from a lack of exposure to and interaction with people of a particular background. Increased interaction with them can often overcome bias, as people come to know and respect each other. If the bias involves race, then it is especially difficult for the community organizer, who may well abandon the seemingly futile project instead of working through the situation.

It helps to remember that bias is a universal and necessary human condition. We are all biased. If we were not biased, then we would go through life having to independently assess and react to each and every change in the condition of each and every aspect of whatever circumstance we find ourselves in. Our daily lives are filled with assumptions, many of which are based on biases that guide our action and inactions. To quote from Gordon Allport's seminal work on the subject, *The Nature of Prejudice*:

> The human mind must think with the aid of categories. Once formed, categories are the basis for normal prejudgment. We cannot possibly avoid this process. Orderly living depends upon it.[64]

By way of example, you enter a subway car. There are few seats available and the most convenient one is near a young man who is taking up more than one seat, playing music that can be heard through his headphones, with legs wide open and his book bag on the space next to him. Assuming there are other, though not as convenient, seats in the car, instead of asking him to make room, you would probably assume that he is self-absorbed and inconsiderate, the type who would either resent the suggestion to move over or would outright resist it. So, instead, you sit in a less convenient area of the subway car or you simply stand. We habitually make assumptions based on the age, demeanor, dress, race or ethnic background of the person. If the young person in the subway car looks like our best friend's son, we might be more inclined to ask that he make room.

Here's another example. If you are driving into a parking lot of a mall in the late afternoon and the nearest available space is next to a group of teenagers who are socializing, although not in any openly threatening manner, you would probably drive on. You would likely assume: (1) they might be rowdy; (2) they might sit on your car after it is parked; (3) they might be drinking or engaging in some activity that may cause problems; (4) they might become raucous and bump into you or your car; (5) they might be rude… and so on. These assumptions manifest a genuine bias against congregating youth. And most of us would act upon this bias by driving further than is convenient, away from the group of ordinary teens.

---

[64] Gordon W. Allport, *The Nature of Prejudice*, Perseus Books, 1979, p. 20. Allport also makes reference to Bertram Russell, "…a mind perpetually open will be a mind perpetually vacant."

Consider an alternative approach to the parking scenario: you drive slowly into the space next to the teenagers. You get out of the car and attempt to interview each of the teenagers about their backgrounds, experiences, educational experiences, family lives, morals, religious beliefs, and so on – all for the purpose of replacing your blind assumptions with a more thorough understanding of these kids so you can make a more educated decision as to whether or not to park in the most available and convenient parking space. After you have completed the individual assessments, you then proceed to ascertain if there are any particular group dynamics that would cause you concern, which requires speaking to the youth as a group. After this, assuming that it could be done to your satisfaction before midnight, you then have to finesse the sidewalk, the front door, salespersons, other customers, unattended children, etc.

Certainly, some bias is necessary to get us through the day. Too often, however, we attempt to shelter ourselves through our environment and affiliations so we do not encounter unfamiliar people or circumstances at all.

The Comfort of the Familiar. Up until recently, I had two dogs who were brother and sister. My wife and I got these dogs from our veterinarian on the Grand Concourse in the Bronx in the mid-nineties. Both dogs were very small and very sick at the time. But they recovered and went on to lead very active lives, always in the other's company and always with the female in the lead. ("Just as it should be," joked my wife.) They were always together, the female always taking care of her brother. In 2004, Penney developed pancreatic cancer and died. Afterwards, Petey was alone for the first time in his life. He stopped eating. He became scared of everything: the doorbell, the telephone, other dogs. He was unable to function, and my wife and I realized that with the loss of his dominant sister, a dominance from which he obviously took comfort, Petey felt he had lost control of his environment.

Humans seek to be in control of our environments, and we often prefer to be with others like ourselves. In that way, we have an easier job managing our everyday affairs. The people that we see look like us; they speak our language; they share our customs; appreciate our mutual heritage; have values in common, and so on. In our everyday affairs, we feel that our beliefs, our lifestyles, our choices, our priorities, our viewpoints, are constantly being supported. And this makes us secure and happy.

The problem is that our reaction is often extreme when the conditions of that environment change – new neighbors move in, people speak in a foreign language, kids from another neighborhood are bused in, etc. Essentially, we feel threatened by that which is changed around us. Much like my dog who was dysfunctional once his sister died, people in these changing circumstances will often find themselves unable to cope. These people often react in irrational anger or become more and more insulated and withdrawn. The alternative is to open up and take the risks, including rejection, inherent in exposing oneself to others. This is more likely to succeed with the intervention of a third party, such as a minister or a community organizer.

Prejudice. Prejudice is the manner in which we act out our biases each day. Two people who are openly biased can work through those biases and cooperate with one another as long as they are not vested in, and part of, a racist environment. But the perspectives and assumptions of each of the individuals must be openly discussed through experiences shared in a non-threatening, neutral environment.

One of the more frustrating aspects of community development and organizing is that most people adamantly choose not to participate in any mutual exercise, even if apparently beneficial. This prejudicial behavior is debilitating. It means we are choosing to protect our bias at all costs, even while living within an environment that places our bias at a disadvantage. Bias has the dual capacity of becoming either hardened over time or of maturing over time, depending on how secure we feel and how open we are to change, which is always threatening to some degree.

When in our everyday lives we confront changes we cannot accommodate, prejudice will occur, a sign that our bias is either out of line with our environment or (if we are beyond adapting at that point) that the environment is becoming more and more antagonistic to our emotional existence. It is at this point that our bias may become activated in our daily lives and find expression in pervasive prejudice, as personified in the popular television character Archie Bunker.

Though difficult, prejudice can be managed, ameliorated and even eliminated, at any point in time and within a set of circumstances. This is one of many primary challenges for community organizers, a challenge that cannot be taken lightly, and a challenge that with certain individuals, may be insurmountable.

Racism. Racism is the extreme manifestation of racial bias and prejudice in a systematic fashion, and with institutional support (community, organization, religious affiliation, etc.) for the purpose helping one preferred group, and with the corollary purpose of hurting another group. Racism can be acted out individually or as a group. However, as with any "ism," racism must exist as a prevailing condition for it to be acted out either individually or collectively, whether or not that behavior is pursuant to informal social norms or publicly-sanctioned legality. Racism is a part of our society to the extent that individual prejudice is institutionalized through social norms, accepted conventions, legal sanctions, economic practices, or political processes.

In the United States, "practiced" racism is, for the most part, illegal. However, this illegality extends back only a few decades. Before that, racism was inherent in the federal system of providing mortgage insurance for home purchases where title excluded blacks and other minorities. This practice was more than just the acceptance of private practices and conventions: the promotion of racial segregation was actively practiced as a federal policy. The purported purpose was to promote racially harmonious communities, supposedly possible only through the exclusion of minorities from white communities. These practices permeated the legal, finance and real estate professions. The practice was somewhat circumscribed by the 1948 case of Shelley v. Kraemer, 334 U.S. 1 (1948), which prohibited state enforcement of racially restrictive covenants, but the ruling did not rule out the use of such covenants, which contained written notice of who was welcome and who was not welcome within certain communities. The practice of allowing restrictive racial covenants in deeds continued until the Fair Housing Act of 1968.

Before that, the following restrictive property covenant was typical and fully operative:

> ... and that no building erected upon said premises[65] shall ever be used for the sale of liquor, wine or beer or be rented wholly or in part to or occupied by negroes or colored persons... and further that this covenant against nuisances shall attach and run with the land.

So there you have it: a human being of color defined as a "nuisance," lumped into the category of vices brought about by alcoholic beverages.

Racism is not always expressed so starkly. Sometimes it is more indirect. One could certainly argue that it is racist to target flight paths over minority neighborhoods. The reason most often cited for this practice is that controllers are told to avoid flying over neighborhoods that are organized, that vote, and that complain about the flights. It just so happens that those organized communities are mainly white.

"Environmental Racism." Racism can take subtle forms. Take the recent concept of "environmental racism." Whether it be a drug rehab center, a juvenile detention center, a homeless shelter, or a garbage incinerator, any unpopular facility is almost always sited in a low-income, minority community. On the surface, this appears to fit the definition of racism, especially with respect to such facilities as garbage incinerators, given the extraordinary incidence of asthma in inner city communities such as the South Bronx.

One could argue that the decision to site is simply a matter of availability (more vacant land), economics (the city owns much of the vacant land in inner city areas so that there is no cost of acquisition), and political expediency (no need for eminent domain). When the New York City Charter was radically amended in 1989, a small group of advocates (myself included) fought for its

---

[65] 450 West 131st Street, New York, N.Y., which is now a Section 202, CATCH senior housing project named "Logan Gardens," inhabited mostly by African Americans and named after a civil rights pioneer, Dr. Arthur Logan, a prominent black surgeon in New York City.

rejection. Once we lost that battle, we decided to work on the rulemaking side of the struggle since rules (regulations) can make a bad law into tolerable law, just as they can make a good law intolerable. In the original draft of the "Fair Share" rules that dealt with the siting of facilities, the language of the rules made cost a pre-eminent factor in these decisions. Because we knew that low cost would always tilt the decision-making towards inner-city communities of color where there were still large banks of free, city-owned land, we fought for and won the requirement that city agencies must openly consider other factors and include weighing the cost and benefits of a private "taking" of property against the cost and benefits of using publicly-owned land. Recently, the city was prepared to do just that – use its eminent domain power to obtain an 11-acre, privately owned site for the construction of a 2000-bed jail. Ironically, the private site is located in the Hunts Point area of the South Bronx, an area starved for parkland and waterfront access, with two existing youth detention facilities (one that was supposed to be closed over a decade ago) and a floating jail barge.

Power and Racism. Racism pre-supposes power.[66] Racism represents the acting out of bias within a system that officially promotes that action and results in harm to a racial group. Racism is, by definition, an exercise of power. So some black activists and intellectuals say that blacks cannot be racist because they lack power within the dominant political system.

This sentiment assumes that the "dominant political system" is a unitary, non-divisible political manifestation, and that it is the only system within which racism can be exercised. But this belief ignores the fact that within the "dominant political system" there are innumerable smaller, interacting, and subordinated political systems. For example, a single block in Harlem, in New York City, can possess all the social dynamics to permit the exercise of collec-

---

[66] See Hannah Arendt's explanation of the origin of power in her book, *On Revolution,* Op. cit., "power comes into being only if and when men join themselves together for the purpose of action… binding and promising, combining and covenanting are the means through which power is kept in existence…" p.175.

tive power and racism – against whites. This can be exhibited by the systematic denial of housing and social assistance (such as the simple denial of providing directions or purposefully providing the wrong directions).

Some years ago, the New York State Department of Motor Vehicles developed a racist dynamic in several of its New York offices. I first became aware of this when my 18-year-old brother-in-law got his driving license. Since he lived with our family, I was amazed to learn that he knew how to drive. As it turned out, he did not: he had simply purchased his license from a Bronx motor vehicle office. We learned that several such offices were in the business of selling licenses and other services to minorities. Blacks had to pay a nominal fee; Hispanics had to pay a little more; and Asians had to pay the most. As for whites, they were not allowed to purchase licenses at all and had to tolerate antagonistic service, perhaps to get them to go to another motor vehicle office.

Whites had the inconvenience of having to go elsewhere for services, while the other groups were put in danger by receiving licenses for which they were not qualified. About a month after obtaining his license, my brother-in-law totaled his car when he drove it into a pole in Hunts Point. Luckily, he was uninjured. The sale of licenses to blacks, Hispanics, and Asians, at different price levels, was clearly the exercise of racism within a closed system, although upon analysis, it is clear that all groups were harmed. Indeed, every member of the general public was endangered by the selling of licenses to non-drivers.

Anti-White Racism and CATCH. A few years ago, CATCH was about to sponsor its first tax credit project in Harlem. This was a big deal for the organization since it involved multiple buildings that would receive substantial renovation funds and allow the units to remain affordable for its members, virtually all of whom were black. We were already involved in four buildings in the neighborhood through the Central Harlem MHA – the corporation that owned these buildings and was governed by the residents themselves.

Community Board 10 in Harlem held a public hearing on the new project. And even though I was urged not to attend, I resisted the advice on the grounds that I was the President of CATCH, the sponsor group, and owed it to the community board to show up personally and present the project.

It was all downhill from there. Here was a group of black leaders who only saw a white man with an office in downtown Manhattan. Nothing I could say about our past work, my own background, or our ongoing involvement with resident-controlled housing in Harlem could shake these community representatives from their own prejudices. The board voted down the project.

Not long after, we held a Central Harlem MHA board meeting to discuss strategy. We settled on meeting with a local elected official who would get us back on the next Community Board 10 agenda, which he did.

At that meeting, one after the other, our local MHA leaders went to the microphone to speak. Each one of them lectured the board, demanding that they explain what gave them the right to decline these needed funds and further challenging the board members to explain where they were when they needed help. Marcia Evans, President of the Central Harlem MHA, related the story of her wall that was separating from the building, causing the NYC Buildings Department to nearly place a vacate order on the building. "CATCH was there to help us. Where were you?" Kirwin Stewart spoke about the bank foreclosure and the residents' fear that the building would be auctioned to speculators and the residents displaced. "CATCH was there. Where were you?" And so it went through about 10 speakers, all CATCH and local MHA members and leaders.

The members of the Community Board became so flustered that they started arguing amongst themselves, with some charging others with being racist. At one point, one light-skinned African American proclaimed that if we thought we would get this project approved, "You can kiss my black ass." To which another board member replied, "Your ass ain't so black!" This all happened on the record at a public meeting! This time, the project was approved.

Racism and Anti-Racism. The topic of racism can be very confusing. Within any given society, those who seem openly racist can take up the arguments of anti-racists and seemingly justify racism – effectively standing liberal, anti-liberal arguments on their heads.

This phenomenon was described in some detail by Pierre-André Taguieff, as "racism and its doubles."[67] Essentially, he frames the problem as follows:

> ... racism and antiracism risk admitting positions of discourse that today have become indiscernible, mimetically accepting the same primary and positive value of difference and sacralization.[68]

What he means by the above jargon-filled analysis is that there is a basic antinomy – two equally defensible and legitimate theses that are irreconcilable – in the antiracist dialogue and action against "racism." On one side, there is the argument for human rights that focuses on the individual as an individual and a member of "humanity." On the other side, there is the argument of the traditionalist protector of ethnic differences and culture. Just as the anti-racist humanist might say that we must respect differences and work to preserve cultural differentiation, the racist can defend his racism on the grounds that differences matter and that the only way to preserve culture is to treat different ethnic and cultural groups differently. Thus the protection of one or another race becomes a legitimate public purpose.

And just as another anti-racist humanist might say that we should all be "color-blind" and treat all as equals ("we are all humans" or "we are all children of God"), the racist can say that all forms of government assistance are wrong, since we should all be treated equally, without recognition of social, economic, and barriers to equality.

In its more conventional form, racism is easier to identify and to combat. Racist dialogue was originally not so much against another group or groups as it was an exhibition of pride and ethnic affiliation, as in "France for the French." However, as this ethnic pride took on anthropological dimensions and developed towards extreme nationalism, such as pan-Germanism, racism developed into the grotesque phenomenon of National Socialism, a form of ra-

---

[67] Pierre-André Taguieff, *The Force of Prejudice, On Racism and Its Doubles*, The University of Minnesota Press, 2001.
[68] *Ibid*, p. 80.

cism based upon "self-racialization.[69]" Under this form of racism, there is a recognition of difference based upon genetics, which leads to the felt need for purification and extermination of those outside the ideal gene pool. This form of extreme racism is easy to abhor because it is so obviously evil and repugnant, yet it is still being practiced as "ethnic cleansing" in Eastern Europe, the Mideast, and Africa.

Taguieff's book is a rather depressing tome, since it seems that no matter which way we turn, we are faced with an emerging contradiction, a problem exploited by the "New Right" in France. However, both Taguieff and Allport provide some guidance for escaping this dilemma. Both take the position that you cannot legislate away prejudice or racism and beyond that they offer similar approaches. I believe their point has merit. For example, you can outlaw restrictive racial covenants in deeds, but you cannot outlaw private, gated communities. You can outlaw "separate but equal" educational facilities, but you cannot outlaw private schools. You can outlaw discrimination in the allowed use of public amenities, but you cannot outlaw private country clubs or even municipal priorities that allow public places to fall into disrepair. You can outlaw unequal delivery of public services, but you cannot outlaw the diminishing of public services, which will most hurt those who cannot afford to provide those services for themselves.

Practicing Patience. Allport supports the freedom to assimilate or not to assimilate, as each individual desires. He states that this should be the choice of the person belonging to the minority group.[70] The majority needs to practice patience and exhibit relaxed and permissive attitudes towards those who are in a position to assimilate or preserve cultural and ethnic identity. According to Allport, it may be more "effective to help an individual gain in self-esteem than

---

[69] *Ibid*, p.120.
[70] Allport, G. Op. cit., p. 240.

to try to raise his respect for others."[71] For "the development of mature and democratic personalities is largely a matter of building inner security."[72]

Taguieff focuses on the need for public space[73], communication, a *de jure* unity of humanity and the ability to live with contradictions. He urges us not to apply energy towards racists, but rather to learn to live with the contradictions and to do good work in areas of human interaction that are accessible to us.[74] He makes further reference to philosophy and ethics to guide our approach. For example, he states that we should stop viewing individuals as means and see each person as an "end" in and of him or herself. He exhorts us not to love one another as oneself, but rather to love another before oneself. He makes reference to Kant's distinction between price and dignity, in that humans should each have a non-diminishable dignity that cannot "admit of equivalents." These and other prescriptions seem very idealistic and rather unconvincing.

In the end, these authors seem to agree that racism is multi-faceted, complex, and universal. They say we need to recognize the problem but not be daunted by its complexity. And if the law cannot prescribe (only proscribe), then perhaps it is up to society to reconcile the tension.

So what is the best medium through which to work through these very complex issues within society? I maintain that geographic communities are the most productive starting point for dealing with this problem, even acknowledging that communities tend more towards exclusivity than inclusiveness. Only communities, which foster interdependence and interconnectedness, can provide the setting for working through the complex and destructive realities of bias, prejudice and racism.

---

[71] *Ibid*, p.388.
[72] *Ibid*, p. 441.
[73] Taguieff, P. Op. cit., p.311.
[74] *Ibid*, p. 298.

XI Economics and the Inner City Community

No community development effort can be undertaken in a vacuum. Understanding the economic dynamics of a particular area is as important as understanding its political, social, and historical circumstances. Economic circumstances include access to jobs and business opportunities and the social and cultural barriers to such access. Understanding the economic background and history of an inner city or impoverished rural area is crucial for the community organizer because economic research can be an important part of advocacy.

Blaming the Poor. When Ronald Reagan became President in 1981, the country was in the middle of a recession, inflation was out of control, and working people throughout the country, especially whites, were susceptible to speeches by elected leaders who blamed economic problems on those receiving public benefits. The President talked about "welfare queens" using their food stamps to buy vodka, and many people wanted to believe that this sort of thing was the general rule for all welfare recipients. Why? Because it is simpler to blame a class of people for the woes of the many than to look to more complex, systemic problems. Besides, it is easy to tap into biases held by many, to formalize those biases through direct public sanction, and to convert the biases (dormant) into prejudices (active). From there, it is easy to make public policy that blames the poor and does not provide them with needed benefits.

Research is an indispensable component of advocacy, organizing, and development because it can provide the rationale for new positions and outcomes. It is also a necessary precedent to any action seeking to change public policy because organizers need to overcome pervasively held biases that, without research, prevent humane changes in public policy.

For example, there is the pervasive belief in this country that the poor are lazy and are directly responsible for their own bleak circumstances. This belief allows us to decide that there is no need for us to take personal or public responsibility for the poor. The Republican Party has raised to an art form the practice of making generalizations about all poor people from extraordinary exceptions (as Ronald Reagan's welfare queens) and then blaming the poor for their own problems. To this day, it is no accident that conservative religious groups have great influence on a political party that stresses personal responsibility and a secularized version of divine providence. Those who are fortunate have gotten what they have worked for and deserve: they are blessed by God. Those who are unfortunate have caused their own problems by not taking personal responsibility for their own needs: they have failed to heed their station and rejected God's will.

Such religious sentiments raise "Divine Providence" to a new level.[75] The more recent popular secular theory embodied in the "laws of attraction"[76] holds that, rather than God's grace rewarding the worthy, good (and bad) things come through the power of thought. According to *The Secret*, if someone has problems, it is once again his or her own fault. If someone is "blessed" it is due to the objective, universal and pervasive "laws of attraction," which bring good things to those who think good thoughts, and bad things to those who think bad thoughts.

---

[75] See Max Weber, *The Protestant Work Ethic and the Spirit of Capitalism*, Chapter 5: "A specifically bourgeois economic ethic has grown up. With the consciousness of standing in the fullness of God's grace and being visibly blessed by Him... Finally, it gave him the comforting assurance that the unequal distribution of [wealth] ... was a special dispensation of Divine Providence." Source: Routledge Classics, Taylor & Francis Group, 2001, p. 120.

[76] Rhonda Byrne, *The Secret*, Atria Books/Beyond Words (2006).

The very fact that *The Secret* can be a bestseller shows that we are dangerously close to becoming a people lacking empathy and compassion – a society of self-righteous, narcissistic egotists.

"Command" Economies. When I was in college, I majored in economics, long known as "the dismal science." At that time, we mostly studied so-called free-market economics. When we ventured into the realm of "political economy," the principle subject was communism. We were taught that a command economy such as communism was subject to political (mis-)management and was terribly inefficient, and I never doubted these "truths." By contrast (we were told), the United States and other democratically-housed western economies flourished through the laws of the free market, with a level playing field, an open flow of information, and no overriding political influences. True, there were often disruptions, dislocations and political missteps, causing downturns in the economy, but given the free flow of information, the equitable access to necessary resources, a fair tax policy, and benign government regulation, these temporary problems would self-correct, and the free market would adjust and continue to function effectively and efficiently.

Today, however, it is apparent to me that in the United States we live within a political economy. The form of political economy is different from the command economies of communist countries because the "command" in the United States comes from the needs of private sector as opposed to coming from the needs deemed essential by political bureaucrats, as in communism. In fact, as government policy under George W. Bush tends increasingly towards the promotion of enhanced profit and wealth concentration (as of this writing), it would appear that many of the more people-friendly policies developed in the past are viewed as no longer necessary. Even though the war in Iraq, Katrina, government scandals, and manifest incompetence have temporarily halted the recent trend of using government policy to essentially sell off the public sector and redistribute wealth and power to the already rich, this ongoing shift will probably continue for sometime with only a temporary disruption. Even with the election of a Democrat in 2008, as long as Democrats simultaneously promote both progressive social policies and the caveat that such policies must be revenue neutral (meaning that they have to pay for themselves from spending cuts or tax increases), this trend will likely prevail.

Once again, in the first decade of the 21st Century (as in the eighties), the public sector, through the government's tax and foreign policy, is being bankrupted, and private wealth is being increased at the expense of the working and middle classes.

All of this is possible because of two things. First, our political system is run by elected officials beholden to concentrated wealth and private power (the power to invest, lend, hire, fund a campaign, relocate jobs, advance or squash technology, share information, etc.). Second, we are only a formal democracy – as opposed to a substantive democracy. We have the power to vote, but little power to choose the candidates, who are totally dependent upon the wealthy and the powerful. You need a lot of money to mount a political campaign.

Economics: A Contrived Science. In many ways, economics is a false science or, at the very least, a contrived science. To prove a result, we create abstract paradigms to show that based on innumerable variables pursuant to mathematically-determinable functions, and subject to objective and so-called natural laws of supply and demand, the contrived result is the correct result. Furthermore, no economic research would command much financial support (through research grants, editorial board positions, or the employment of the researcher) if it contradicted the underpinning of our current political economy. So what represents itself as mainstream economic analysis is for the most part a rationalization for a political economy that favors concentration of wealth and the wage and increasing debt enslavement of the vast majority of the population.

The Geo-Political Reality. At its core, economics derives from some geopolitical reality. There needs to be a fixed geographical setting. This fixed setting can be a small piece of land capable of sustaining minimal human needs. Beyond that, it can be a town, a city, or a nation. Beyond the fixed geographical setting, there needs to be a political system capable of "controlling" the behavior of its participants. The system of control can be voluntary, as in a community setting. Only in a community-like setting can there be true democratic self-determination, where the political aspects of economy extend no further than establishing rules, ensuring an equitable sharing of burdens, preventing and punishing abuses, and promoting common goals.

Of course, the system can be totally non-voluntary, as was the case in the USSR. Such an involuntary system was necessary to maintain the centralized political system because it was not possible to centrally command such a huge economy in a democratic fashion. But involuntary systems do not have to be absolute in order to be substantially or effectively involuntary.

If the citizens of a democratic country are manipulated, as opposed to being controlled, then the result can be similar to that in a totalitarian regime. If we have seemingly unlimited consumer choices; if we have the ability to be distracted through seemingly unlimited entertainment media; if we have little or no real interdependence (connection) with neighbors who are not doing well while most of us are not threatened with starvation or homelessness, then a largely undemocratic system can work. Such a political system can function and thrive, even if the system exists far from the democratic ideal.

By way of illustration, picture a central point from which a leash is controlling a person, with the controller shouting out commands and tugging or releasing tension to modify behavior. That provides a simplistic version of an economic system that is involuntary: say the system that existed in the USSR. Now imagine the same person free to move about, but in a limited space, with some options -- but options that are prescribed and limited. This can be seen as a simplistic version of our free, voluntary system in the USA today.

Big-Picture Decisions. With any economic system, the real issue boils down to one thing: how is this specific political system going to organize itself, marshal its resources, decide on common goals, define the common good, and create the rules by which wealth is created, managed, employed, stored, and distributed amongst its members. What means will it use: taxation and direct wealth transfer? Taxation and public provision of services? No taxation and total reliance on cooperation or private charity?

Once such "big picture" decisions are made, it's important to know who makes the decisions necessary to operate the system on an ongoing basis. It is not vital to know *how* the decisions are made. By knowing *who* benefits from the decisions, it is possible to determine who is ultimately responsible for those decisions.

Until recently, this was not obvious. Lines separating the public from the private sectors seemed to be sacrosanct. But now it seems the lines are not only blurring but disappearing altogether.

At the start of the George W. Bush administration, Vice President Cheney invited industry leaders, including the nation's leading polluters, to help make environmental policy. Such arrogance should be extremely disturbing not only to liberals and progressives but to conservatives as well. People in such high positions of power are supposed to be more subtle. For example, Vice President Cheney was supposed to have underlings at the EPA or Department of Energy put together a panel of scientists from major universities. Of course, funding for research at these universities comes from very same titans of the energy industry that Cheney met with to begin with. These scientists, based upon "objective" research involving the most stringent scientific evidence, are then supposed to either prove the political point sought to be made or disprove or cast doubt on some politically inconvenient scientific conclusion or issue, such as global warming.

Armed with these findings, paid lobbyists are supposed to scale the steps of Capitol Hill and convince legislators to support legislation or promote pro-industry regulations. Bolstered by these "scientific" findings, the legislators hold hearings where the same and other experts testify and eventually pass laws that help the same private interests that eventually fund their campaigns. That is how it is supposed to work. Through arrogance or impatience, Vice President Cheney decided to cut through the whole sordid mess and simply held a meeting with the country's major energy producers and decided that he had the right to keep the proceedings secret. I regard Cheney as a major threat and enemy of popular democracy, but sometimes I wonder if we should thank him (I am being facetious) for saving so much money (which would have been otherwise spent on suspect research grants, administering and staffing scientific panels, publication costs, lobbying fees, superfluous campaign contributions) – money that eventually would be borne by the taxpayers.

It is possible to speculate on other, more devious reasons for the extreme secrecy of these Cheney meetings, which may likely have featured agenda related to the provision of very lucrative contracts to selected U.S. companies, such as Halliburton, and the invasion of Iraq to preclude Saddam Hussein from granting major oil concessions to companies from Europe and Asia rather than those from the United States.

Cheney's secret meetings, beyond providing great frustration for those who take the role and responsibility of democratic government seriously, illustrate that those in the field of community development work within an economic, social and political system that is mostly antagonistic to their aims. And even though recognition of macro-economic forces can be depressing to the point of debilitation, it is necessary to have a world view in order to organize anything, even tenants in one building. Notwithstanding the constraints presented by the larger picture, research into economic circumstances is critical to many low-income community advocacy and planning efforts and can often lead to desired results, especially at the local level. What follows is an example of one such effort.

Research Leading to Policy. In the mid-1970s, a group of advocates was struggling with public policy regarding the tens of thousands of units of low-income housing that the city had taken ownership of through proceedings in which properties were foreclosed for failure to pay real estate taxes (*in rem* proceedings*).* "*In rem*" refers to a legal procedure that is taken "against the thing," as opposed to a legal procedure that is against a person, *"in personam."* In these *in rem* proceedings, the City of New York took title to property in tax arrears. Through this policy, New York City had become a reluctant landlord to tens of thousands of low-income households.

Real estate tax collections – the single largest source of revenue to the City – fell to historic lows. One response to the loss of real estate taxes by the city was to pass Local Law 45 of 1976, called the "quick vesting law." This new law permitted the foreclosure of properties for non-payment of real estate taxes after only four quarters of arrears (a single year). Through this law, the city tried to spur landlords to pay their taxes, but instead of paying up, the landlords simply abandoned the buildings. This resulted in a major new housing program – the *In Rem* Housing Program.

In the mid 1970s, housing abandonment in New York City reached its peak. Units were being lost to arson, decay and disinvestment at the astounding rate of 3,300 apartments per month. To understand the scope of this problem, a year's worth of such abandonment approaches in scale the entire population of many of our moderate sized cities in the United States, such as Syracuse, New York or Dayton, Ohio. A major economic factor leading to large scale abandonment was the rise in energy prices for property owners. In a mere fourteen years, from 1967-1981, energy costs rose 733%.

For about a decade – from about 1977 to the late-eighties – there was a window of opportunity for deciding how the city would maintain, upgrade, and eventually dispose of this housing, which at one point represented one of the largest systems of public housing in the country, second only to the New York City Housing Authority.

To help frame policy, we needed both advocacy and a policy framework. A report was commissioned to provide just that. Sponsored by the New York Urban Coalition, *The New York City In Rem Housing Program, A Report* was published in 1985. It had three chapters and a set of recommendations. As Vice President and CEO of the Consumer-Farmer Foundation, Inc. (now the Parodneck Foundation, which was created in 1970 to provide financial and technical assistance to self-help housing and community development efforts throughout New York City's inner city areas), I wrote the first chapter, which attempted to trace the *in rem* crisis through economic and demographic changes over the past three decades. Joan Allen, a friend who was also one of the pioneers at Peoples Development Corporation in the South Bronx in their seventies heyday, wrote the second chapter, a comprehensive analysis of past and then-current *in rem* housing programs. I then wrote the third chapter, which looked at current economic trends. I concluded that the city needed to maintain the tens of thousands of *in rem* units as a public resource, whether administered directly by the city or by the not-for-profit sector. I pointed to studies that indicated that the private sector would increasingly focus on the small, more affluent households, leaving the larger, less affluent, households without adequate housing options.

The committee established to review the report, used it to present public policy recommendations to the City, and community advocates used it for their own work. (Further recommendations and the subsequent results are detailed later in this chapter.)

The Inner City Loses Its Vitality. Historically, the inner city was a place of opportunity. Low paying, entry level jobs (mostly manufacturing) abounded locally or within reach of the working class by way of city mass transit. But this economic paradigm began to erode after the Second World War as the economy became more global. Manufacturing jobs left the Northeast cities, including New York, for points south and, ultimately, east – Far East. Service industries began to overtake manufacturing as the dominant form of economic activity in the city. The jobs in the so-called FIRE sector (Finance, Insurance and Real Estate) paid very well but were not available to the average inner city dweller.

Concurrently, the availability of cars and the development of highways provided an opportunity for suburban development that extended New York City's economy well beyond the political reach of New York City's tax-levy authority. As a result, even as the regional economy grew, New York City itself became poorer and the inner city became a repository for people with ever more limited economic options. More often than not, these people were dependent upon the public sector for support.

The high cost of capital, labor and materials depressed the construction of unsubsidized housing, reducing production to half the level of the previous decade. In 1973, for the first time since World War II, median family income in New York City failed to rise in real dollars. The income of New York City renters actually declined by almost 16% between 1970 and 1976, while rent levels for the first time rose at a rate that outstripped incomes. To my knowledge, this had never been the case before.

In the late seventies, New York City was in the midst of a severe fiscal crisis, with bankruptcy a persistent threat. Credit through the normal channels was unavailable. The city terminated thousands of employees. This point is important because the War on Poverty programs effectively cushioned the loss of private sector jobs in New York City by allowing local governments to increase their payrolls through direct federal grants. In some Model Cities programs, for example, there was a subsidiary service department in addition to the regular municipal service department, such as the Model Cities sanitation division, operating alongside the regular sanitation department.

In the postwar period, there was a dramatic change in the ethnic composition of New York City. Such transformations are not new for New York City, nor indeed for any international city. Unfortunately, the crisis of the mid-seventies occurred as a growing and mostly minority population fed into a city that had a deteriorating economic base and housing stock.

Changing Demographics. In 1950, New York was a city of close to 7.9 million people, of which 90% were white and less than 10% were African-American. By 1976, the year that the New York City fiscal crisis came to a head, blacks and Hispanics constituted nearly 42% of the population. Even as this new minority came into the city, the economy began to shrink, and the new immigrants were left with diminished job opportunities.

For most of its history, New York City functioned as an economic entity largely within its own political boundaries. But with the post-War public development of highways, bridges, tunnels, along with the subsidization of suburban homes, the economic reality of New York City now extended to an entire metropolitan area. A majority of its workforce could now, theoretically, reside outside the city, out of the reach of New York City's taxing authority with regard to sales, real estate and other "use" taxes. So as the New York metropolitan area grew in GNP, New York City's tax authority diminished.

In 1950, New York City's population was still swollen with those who had relocated to the city to take advantage of its wartime production economy. The war was a time of planned production, overtime, austerity and forced consumer saving. Individual savings accounts provided the basis for mortgage financing. Households would save money and receive a small return in the form of interest. The funds were secure through federal deposit insurance, and banks loaned these funds at higher interest rates for longer periods to first-time and other homebuyers. Many of these homebuyers were buying homes in the suburbs.

Taken alone, a federal policy geared to suburban development would suggest a rapid decline in the city population. But this did not happen for a number of reasons, including the migration of Puerto Ricans to the "mainland" – and primarily New York City. Throughout the 1960s and 1970s, the island's formal economy grew at an average of about 6% annually. Nonetheless, half of the island's population remained impoverished, and over 600,000 felt compelled to migrate to the mainland. In addition, in the immediate post-war period, African-Americans from the south continued to migrate north in search of jobs and dignity, for Southern racism was demoralizing and occasionally lethal. By 1970, in spite of a massive out-migration of residents of European descent, New York's population was still 7.9 million.

The Transformation of the New York City Economy. At the height of the New York City fiscal crisis, local officials maintained that the outflow of industry had cost the city hundreds of thousands of manufacturing jobs from the mid-sixties through the mid-seventies. These lost jobs represented, for the most part, entry level positions within the job market. Opportunities for such jobs decreased at exactly the same time that the city's new waves of immigrants were in need of such work.

What follows are a number of charts that I developed to elaborate on what I described as an "opportunity index." These figures were taken or derived, through straight line analysis, from the U.S. Census and were included in the report: *The New York City In Rem Housing Program: A Report.*

Entry Level Job Opportunities in New York City by Sector and Year

Manufacturing					
1954	**1959**	**1963**	**1967**	**1972**	**1977**
947,841	936,492	927,413	852,074	757,900	609,700
Retail					
1954	**1959**	**1963**	**1967**	**1972**	**1977**
399,371	401,321	402,882	395,341	385,915	332,166
Selected Services					
1954	**1959**	**1963**	**1967**	**1972**	**1977**
Incl.G.S.	314,668	337,762	360,857	368,907	376,956
Government Services					
1954	**1959**	**1963**	**1967**	**1972**	**1977**
377,219	261,505	304,997	348,448	349,375	350,302
Total					
1954	**1959**	**1963**	**1967**	**1972**	**1977**
1,724,431	1,913,986	1,973,054	1,956,720	1,862,097	1,669,124
Change					
1954	**1959**	**1963**	**1967**	**1972**	**1977**
	11%	3%	(0.8)%	(4.8)%	(10.4)%

Several trends are apparent. The economy was converting from an industrial to a service-based economy. In addition, government employment increased dramatically from the late-fifties through the late-sixties, by about 34%, ameliorating somewhat the shock of the job market transformation, at least until the beginning of the Nixon administration.

Minority Population Statistics in New York City

Ethnicity	1950	1960	1970	1980
Black	747,608	1,087,931	1,668,115	1,767,910
Hispanic	(negligible)	612,574	1,278,630	1,414,328
Asian & Other	27,908	53,392	70,700	141,433
Total	775,516	1,753,896	3,017,445	3,323,671
Change		126%	72%	10%

The "Opportunity Index". From these two tables, a simple comparison can yield an "opportunity index," an analysis that compares the relationship between the growing minority population and the available entry level jobs position. The index is derived by dividing the number of entry level jobs available at any point in time with the minority population to arrive at a theoretical number of positions available per minority resident. This analysis probably understates the problem since many of the better-paying and potential entry level jobs remained filled by those who had left the city for suburbs. In effect, the index provides a kind of "musical chairs" analysis. The new minority populations had to compete with one another, even while they were also competing with those already holding those positions. Furthermore, the historically-white trade unions were not eager to offer employment to minorities. Good union jobs were viewed by members as a legacy to be passed from one generation to the next.

Based upon the above information, in the mid-fifties, there were 1.45 entry-level jobs for each New York City minority resident. By the mid-sixties, there were 0.9 jobs. By the mid-seventies, there were 0.5 jobs for each minority resident. This is a rough, but still useful analysis of why renter incomes were not keeping up with housing costs, which ultimately translate into rents that can be effectively charged in a local market.

New York's Housing Stock. During the years following the Second World War, it was generally acknowledged that housing production lagged well behind need. Even with this lag in production, in 1950 60% of the city's housing stock was less than thirty years old. By the mid-seventies, exactly the opposite was true. Over 60% of the housing stock had been built prior to 1946. These buildings were in serious need of upgrades. But during this period of time, the inner city areas of New York and other cities were subject to disinvestment, deferred maintenance, and other practices for enhancing income flow and minimizing maintenance expenditures. At the same time, landlords were employing techniques for earning tax deductions. Owners often engaged in "mortgage churning," a practice whereby the owner would "sell" a property on paper for an inflated amount, receiving what was seen as the market value as cash, and taking the balance above the market value in paper (as a purchase money mortgage). With this "paper," the new owner could extract as much rental income as possible, but would also have a huge "basis" for depreciating the property and claiming the tax deduction. For example, a $1,000,000 purchase, depreciated over 27.5years, could allow an owner to shelter over $35,000 in income per year (at that time, about three times the nation's 1975 median income).

Because few new affordable rental units were being created, the vacancy rate was very low, around 2%. This led to over-crowded conditions. And although the post-war period was a time of urban renewal, the public sector was not increasing low income housing units. From 1947 through 1967, urban renewal programs in the United Stated demolished over 400,000 low and moderate income units. An additional 500,000 units were destroyed to make way for urban highway construction. Of these nearly one million units of housing destroyed, only a fraction was replaced.

Renter Income and Median Rent. Median renter income in 1950 was about $2,747. In 1960, 1970, and 1976 median renter income had increased to $5000, $7200, and $8900 respectively. However, adjusted for inflation during the same period, median renter income went from $2747 to $4058 to $4464 and then down to $3764 by 1976.

Median rents in the meantime, went from $49 per month in 1950, to $73, $103, to $190 during the same period. Adjusted for inflation, effective rents increased from $49, to $59, to $64, and then to $80. So in real dollars, rents for the 25-year period increased by about 63%, while renter incomes increased by only about 37%. For the six-year period 1970-1976, real rents increased by 25%, while real incomes for median renters decreased by 16%. During this time period, rents rose at a rate that was on average 67% above income. In those days an apartment was considered affordable if it cost 25% or less of one's monthly income: "one week's pay for one month's rent." So during this period, the median rent charged in New York City became *un*affordable to the median renter at exactly the time Local Law 45 was passed in 1976: the legislation that caused the creation of the city's *in rem* housing stock.

This was a remarkable change within just three decades. While I was working on the report and looking at these postwar trends, I decided to look into the relationship between rent and debt service (mortgage payments – the basic way people own homes).

Rents v. Mortgage Payments. At the time, I called up my mother and asked her how difficult it was to go from paying rent to paying debt service when my parents bought a home in the early 1950s. She told me that their monthly mortgage payment was actually cheaper than rent. I was amazed, so I ran some numbers (omitting, for simplicity, the usual down payment) and found that she was right. Taking a median priced home in 1950 ($6,000) at a 4% interest rate yielded debt service of about $37/mth at the time when median rents in New York City were at $49/month. By 1960, this was no longer the case. With a median home in the $16,500 range, debt service would be about $119 (at 6%) while the median rent was $73. By 1984, a median priced home of about $73,000 with a mortgage interest rate of 15% would cost $975 in monthly debt service, as against a median rent of $240. In 1950 debt service stood at about 13.5% of median renter income while by 1980 it stood at almost 90%. Clearly New York City's renters in the mid-seventies were not going to own their homes any time soon.

The Results of the Report. As a result of *The New York City In Rem Housing Program, A Report* and its dissemination, the Parodneck Foundation became viewed as a leader for *in rem* tenants, and *in rem* housing became a long-term affordable housing resource. Among the recommendations that eventually became public policy:

1. Within three years of the report's publication, the City's capital budget became the primary source of upgrading *in rem* housing units.
2. Available federal rental subsidies and eventually the city's allocation of federal tax credits were used in these units of buildings being sold.
3. These units were viewed as a housing resource for homeless families, although it was ultimately concluded that the units were more viable over the long term when their occupants had a mix of incomes.
4. Clusters of buildings were comprehensively renovated for affordable housing, which was incorporated into the Vacant Cluster Program years later.
5. The city increased the allocation of capital funds for the more extensive and comprehensive upgrading of building systems prior to selling properties to tenants, not-for-profit and for-profit groups. Before this, the city had sold buildings after only a minimal amount of renovation, usually enough to pay for only one or two systems upgrades (i.e. roof and boiler).
6. The city continued an aggressive vesting of title for tax delinquent properties through the middle of Mayor Dinkins' term (1991), thus capturing important housing resources prior to their deterioration.
7. The city established the "Ownership Transfer Program" within its development department. Under this program (a kind of "*in rem* prevention program") the city provided loans to groups of residents who worked to purchase their buildings from landlords and turn them into cooperatives.

Of course, many of our recommendations were not implemented:

1. The city did not agree then or at any time that the *in rem* housing stock should be seen, first and foremost as a "public housing resource." At this

writing, the relatively few remaining units are targeted for a sales and rehab program. The city did, however, use its available federal rental subsidies to assist *in rem* properties, although many of those subsidies went to tenants of buildings sold to private owners. In subsequent studies sponsored by the Parodneck Foundation, research showed a demographic "missing middle" in most of the buildings sold to private, for-profit owners, indicating the displacement of then-existing residents in favor of upper income households, on the one hand, and the homeless on the other.[77]
2. The city also did not change its consolidation policy (a policy of emptying out buildings and consolidating residents in less marginal buildings). Rather, it shifted the burden of the relocation of tenants and the redevelopment of partially occupied and vacant buildings to its for-profit and not-for-profit developers.
3. The city never pursued the development of locally-generated plans for the redevelopment of its *in rem* housing. Planning prerogatives were jealously guarded within the city housing agency.
4. After a brief increase in vestings for tax delinquent properties, there was an effective 9-year moratorium on foreclosure for tax arrears between 1991 and 2000. Ultimately, the Giuliani administration changed *in rem* policy by creating two programs, one of which sold tax liens to investment trusts for collection, and eventual auction and sale, and the other of which facilitated transfers to for-profit and not-for-profit "third parties." In this way, the city used its power to foreclose without taking on actual ownership.

All in all, however, the research and advocacy efforts of the Parodneck Foundation were highly worthwhile. *In rem* housing remained an important affordable housing resource for the next 15 to 20 years after the initial 1985 report. This report placed the *in rem* situation within a larger economic context and showed that "personal responsibility" had nothing to do with the problem

---

[77] See *Housing in the Balance: Seeking a Comprehensive Policy for City-Owned Housing*, edited by Michele Cotton, Parodneck Foundation for Self-Help Housing and Community Development, Inc. May, 1993.

of available housing for New York's working class. The economic research that went into the report and the recommendations with which it concluded provided community developers with the facts and figures to justify the preservation of *in rem* housing as an affordable resource for the foreseeable future.

As of this writing, the city's dilemma is: how to produce affordable housing without having a ready resource at its disposal? This is a situation similar to what the city faced in sixties, when there was little if any land to build upon. The important difference now is that rehabilitation is a recognized tool for housing preservation and development. So the city can focus its resources on the preservation and upgrade of its existing stock as it explores ways to expand the housing supply.

XIII Public Policy

Look at almost any piece of legislation and you will find a preamble concerning the bill's background and legislative intent. Some of the most grandiose visions for humankind can be found in these preambles. I remember reading the preamble to the 1970 National Environmental Protection Act and thinking there could be no need for further legislation in this matter: NEPA was going to solve our environmental problems now and for all time.

Legislative acts provide the authority for the implementation of public policy, and by stating the public purpose involved, the preamble to any piece of legislation is used to justify public intervention into the area, as well the public expense.

With the various National Housing Acts of the 1930s through the 1960s, the stated intents were to provide every American with a decent and safe place to live. During the post-World War II era, public sentiment decreed that a decent home was the right of every American, including the poor, who were viewed as the muscle for the ongoing industrial might of the US – the only major industrial nation not to have had battles fought on its mainland. The provision of new homes to returning veterans was a public sentiment and a public policy, as the following preamble testifies:

Harold DeRienzo

Declaration of National Housing Policy
Housing Act of 1949
(Public Law 171, 81st Congress; 63 Stat. 413; 42 U.S.C. 1441)

The Congress hereby declares that the general welfare and security of the Nation and the health and living standards of its people require housing production and related community development sufficient to remedy the serious housing shortage, the elimination of substandard and other inadequate housing through the clearance of slums and blighted areas, and the realization as soon as feasible of the goal of a decent home and suitable living environment for every American family, thus contributing to the development and redevelopment of communities and to the advancement of the growth, wealth, and security of the Nation. The Congress further declares that such production is necessary to enable the housing industry to make its full contribution toward an economy of maximum employment, production and purchasing power.

Unacknowledged Goals of the National Housing Act of 1949. I maintain that many other public policy needs were also being less directly addressed through the Housing Acts.

1. The destruction of dense urban neighborhoods and the dispersal of low-income residents. These neighborhoods were seen as breeding grounds for gangs, social agitation, crime – and organized labor. Those in power were threatened by the labor organizing of the early part of the century and the social agitation of the sixties, so the destruction of neighborhoods housing people calling for political and economic change was probably seen as a worthwhile goal. Dense urban neighborhoods were destroyed in favor of either projects – vertical towers for low-income people – or suburban developments, with single-family, perimeter-fenced homes. Either option provided both a response to left-leaning complaints about the ravages of capitalism (poverty and one of its defining conditions, poor housing), as well as a means towards promoting the "American dream," which features home ownership (with or without the white picket fence). These new housing op-

tions also served to atomize households, further insulating them from potentially popular political movements.
2. Residential access for current and future immigration. Free market experiments like FOMENTO in Puerto Rico could only succeed if immigrants had access to housing. Later waves of immigrants, displaced by globalization, would also need housing.
3. Providing an economic stimulus, through new home building and the construction of highways and suburban infrastructure, to help the US convert from a war-time to a peace-time economy.
4. Prodding the economy towards fuller employment and higher labor participation rates.
5. Expanding the middle class through subsidizing the costs of homeownership through loan guarantees, low interest rates, tax relief for mortgage holders, highway and road development, infrastructure development, and subsidization of utility costs. A middle class expanded through homeownership was seen as a way to promote the Jeffersonian ideal of democracy, supported through the diverse ownership of land. Of course, Jefferson's democratic ideal was based upon diverse land ownership that provided each citizen with the ability to live independently, along with a vested interest in promoting a stable local economic and political system. Homeownership in and of itself, particularly in an era of expanding economic opportunity, also worked to preempt calls for political change and helped maintain the free market system

And that is not all. There was the sense that a healthy population was better provided for in the suburbs than the cities; that the cities were crime-ridden venues with gang-ridden schools; that the US should trumpet the benefits of a pluralistic democracy through high homeownership rates in a bi-polar world that was defined as either "free" or "communist."

As this analysis demonstrates, many goals can be pursued simultaneously through public policy. However, something usually happens after the announcement of a public goal and before the enactment of that goal through legislation.

This "something" is the competition of competing values within our political system, a system that is skewed towards those with money and influence.

When I talk about this in a classroom setting, I find that the following provides a framework for discussion and debate. It helps to demonstrate that rhetoric should be separated from actual intent and outcome. Analyzing who benefits from actual outcomes helps us understand the power arrangements in any political system.

Formulating Public Policy. Public policy formation occurs within a political framework within which decisions are made, programs are developed, and efforts are coordinated among the various sectors – public, private, voluntary. Public policy is often framed as broad-based goals that are widely agreeable, but the resulting legislation is a direct result of the relative power of the sectors and their players. By analyzing the outcomes, as opposed to the proposed intentions of such legislation, it is possible to gain a greater understanding of the power relationships that prevail in any given political system.

What follows is not meant to translate by line across columns, but rather is meant to be reviewed as what makes for non-controversial political platitudes on the one hand (left column) and what results through the political process of exercising power, as it exists at any one time.

The Concept of Community

What Goes In: Stated Policy Goals	What Comes Out: Public Outcomes
Full Employment	Global Free Trade
Right to Work	Government Deficits
Promoting American Business Abroad	Suburbanization
Free Trade/Open Markets	Capital Mobility
Friendly Investment Climate	Destruction of Local Economies
Freedom of Choice	Job Flight
Healthy Population	Centralized Government Power
Equal Opportunity for All	Inequitable Taxation
Affordable, Quality Housing	Loss of Economic Security
Affordable, Quality Health Care	Unaffordable Health Care
Individual Responsibility	Unaffordable Housing
Educated Citizenry	Formalized Democracy
Elimination of Urban Blight	Family as Preferred Social Unit
Ensuring National Security	Bankrupted Local Governments
Consumer Protection	Deregulation
Environmental Protection	Loss of Community
Personal Responsibility	Loss of Individual Liberties

The process outlined above works through a set of competing values and interests that are played out in the public sector. We will list these values later.

The left column of the chart attempts to demonstrate the kinds of public policy goals that politicians and others continually invoke as complementary, comprehensive, and compatible. Little effort is made to explain the inherent problems among goals with competing values, nor is any effort made to justify one over another. For instance, during his terms as President, Bill Clinton would often repeat his overarching goals of promoting "democracy and free trade." Never was there an attempt to suggest that free trade, in its purest form, is anathema to pluralistic democracy.

Over time, I came to interpret the "democracy and free trade" refrain as meaning democracy for transnational corporations, free to transfer capital, technology, information and intellectual property across borders at will and claiming protection from patent infringement, the right to acquire indigenous genetic information, and unfettered access to raw materials and cheap labor. This may seem a cynical analysis, but it is closer to the truth than blithely stating that we can have free markets and (pluralistic) democracy at once.

Very few politicians would say that they are in favor of high unemployment, high interest rates, domestic corporations that are unable to compete globally, weak national security, high taxes, deficient educational opportunities, a degraded environment, and so on. So, politicians usually state that they are in favor of all the goals stated in the left column and, like President Bill Clinton, feel no compelling need to reconcile the competing values and interests that underlie those goals.

Competing Values. Here are some competing values that must be reconciled before the writing of any legislation and that should be part of open and inclusive debate. It is not the purpose here to promote one value over another, but instead to demonstrate two things:

1. In a democracy, competing values should be clearly delineated and vetted, with lines of accountability for the positions taken, and
2. Since these values are competing, a victory for one often comes at the expense of the other, so the ramifications of choosing one value over the other should be explicitly recognized.

Suburban	vs.	Urban
Increasing Wages	vs.	Stable Monetary Policy (i.e. low inflation)
Automobile	vs.	Mass Transit
Local	vs.	Global Economy
Local	vs.	Central Government
National Government	vs.	World Trade Regulations
Community	vs.	Family
Religion	vs.	Individual Rights
Homeownership	vs.	Rental Housing
Private	vs.	Public Wealth
Free Market	vs.	Controlled Markets
Free Market	vs.	Equitable Taxation
Capital	vs.	Labor

Public policy is what results from reconciling these various dyads. It is an extraordinarily complex and dynamic process involving trade-offs at every step of the way. (If there were no trade-offs, there would be no need for a political system.) Obviously, current laws and regulations give priority to the interests of capital over those of labor. If government were organized to serve the interests of labor, then there would be no NAFTA; there would be universal health insurance; jobs would be guaranteed to all those able to work, and no one would work for less than a livable wage. Also, tax policy would be more progressive; there would be no talk of eliminating the capital gains, gift or estate tax, and there would probably be no billionaires. It would not be possible for Lawrence Ellison, of Oracle, to have earned $706 million in one year, as he did in 2001.

American Public Policy. If public policy did not favor suburbs, then government would not subsidize the cost of suburban sprawl. If mass transit was favored, our major rail companies would not go bankrupt every 20 or 30 years, and our fuel costs would be higher, as they are in Europe. If local governance was favored over central governance, federal preemption in areas of trade, commerce and industry would not be so prevalent, and the federal government would not continue to grow in size, even during Republican administrations that champion small government.

Based upon the values that we, as a sovereign nation, hold dearest, we get the outcomes represented in the right hand column of the Rhetoric vs. Outcomes chart. Capital is mobile. To survive, households need to be nearly as mobile as capital. In this country, as in the rest of the world, the industrial sector now offers mainly low-wage jobs. And the low-end service sector offers even lower paying jobs. By contrast, the high-end services sector and the information technology sector can provide lucrative compensation – although even this is beginning to change with the increase in outsourcing. In this country, the automobile reigns supreme among transportation alternatives, in spite of its environmental impact. Communities are dying within a global economy that favors centralized and specialized economies. Corporations and those running them have taken the reigns of political power, while the citizens of this country are provided with infinite consumer choices and multiple avenues for personal gratification. Public education is under-funded, while quality education is available to those able to afford it. Same with healthcare.

A recent issue of *The Economist* carried an ad by an oil company announcing its annual economic essay contest. The contest had one question that went something like, "Should we export jobs or import workers?" Either response ignores unemployed and under-employed US citizens, assuming that these people, presumably without any "personal responsibility," are beyond hope – and certainly beyond training.

My point is that public policy creates very real outcomes over time and it is crucial to participate in the process, even if the deck seems stacked against community interests.

Intermediary Institutions. I mentioned above that government, assisted by intermediary institutions, has the job of mediating among competing interests and ensuring the greatest good for the greatest number. The institutions that serve as intermediaries between government and, say, corporations engaged in international trade, do have a major say in public policy because they have done a good job of making sure that government is organized to serve their interests. However, intermediary institutions that serve those who lack power, as with most community development corporations, are not really intermediary institutions at all. Rather, such CDCs are more "mitigating" institutions, their purpose being to assist those affected by the prevailing political arrangements to adjust to conditions that may not be optimal, or may even be antagonistic.

Forming Public Policy. The first step for a solid community organization is to gain a perspective that allows it to do more than manage crises, transition, and adjustment and instead transform political arrangements to benefit the people it serves. This is no easy task, and charitable foundations are not eager to fund such efforts, but such a perspective must be attempted for a community group to truly be a "community" group.

We still live in an open society. "Reality" is what we make it – it is not some given like death and taxes. Each minute of every day, people are working from the reality of today and building upon it, transforming it to make the reality of tomorrow. There is no "given" in this formula, except for the given that social realities are made by people, not framed by some historical determinism – be it Marxism or corporatist determinism. And it is people who form public policy.

There are two basic ways for citizens to participate in public policy formation. The first involves advocacy around those issues of ongoing priority for the individual and (hopefully) his or her organization. Chances to participate in the formation, development, enhancement, and defense of those issues occur continually. Organized citizens can give public testimony at government forums, participate on panels, prepare research papers, enlist the media, engage in protest, initiate lawsuits, and even lobby elected officials (although tax-exempt organizations do not lobby, they "educate").

The second opportunity comes through participation in some political event of seminal import – a proposed government action that will for the foreseeable future change the rules, the dynamics, the relationships, and the manner in which decisions of public import are made, private activity is or is not regulated and public resources are applied to the formation and execution of public policies. Such a citizen effort might coalesce around the formation of a new school; the new use of a public spaces; or the creation of a new program to implement a newly enacted local law.

The community organizer has a special responsibility to take part in public policy formation. In earlier chapters, I related my experiences in the South Bronx; now I will revisit some of them with regard to public policy formation.

In Rem *Housing*. In 1976, I decided that a section of Kelly Street known as "Banana Kelly" was a good place to take a stand against the arson and abandonment that was devastating the rest of the area. This portion of Kelly Street had three abandoned and vacant buildings (and six occupied adjoining buildings that were owned or managed by the Potts family). Those three vacant buildings became the focus of our development plan – but one of them was privately owned. This was my first substantial and direct experience with the importance of public policy.

The public policy considerations that we had to work through can be outlined as follows:

1. City *In Rem* Policy. The policy at the time that I began organizing on Kelly Street was to take title to tax-delinquent properties after six or more years of tax arrears, and then sell the foreclosed properties at auction. According to then-current policy, we would only be able to gain control of the one privately owned (and abandoned) building on the block by successfully bidding at public auction.
2. City Planning Policy. The planning policy regarding the area at that time was confused, to say the least. Furthermore, the city was broke and had just suspended its Municipal Loan Program, a renovation program for occupied and, to a lesser extent, vacant buildings. Some leaders, such as Roger Starr, former Administrator of the city's housing department, called for "planned

shrinkage," whereby residents from areas of concentrated poverty would be relocated to less "marginal" areas so that the city was planning for its shrinkage, while making it easier and cheaper to deliver services to those in need (regardless of the impact on neighborhoods). Others called for rezoning for industry, others called for a return to agriculture (in the South Bronx!), still others called for suburban-style housing. And, of course, there were those who still called for public housing development.
3. City Acceptance of Squatting/Sweat Equity. At the time we were working on Kelly Street, there was actually a city acceptance of "sweat equity," but there was no program to fund it. "Squatting" was also accepted, although not officially. So at that time, the only way to rehabilitate a building through sweat equity was to work without public funding.
4. City "Preservation" Policy. At the time, if there was no approved funding source for the redevelopment of the property, the city's policy was to demolish that building. One of the three Kelly Street properties was indeed scheduled for demolition.

Kelly Street Victories. In dealing with these policy issues, as a young, politically unsophisticated group, we made lots of mistakes. But in the end we were able to prevail through hard work, insight, planning, cooperation, but most importantly, luck – a confluence of seemingly unrelated factors that came together at just the right time. The real genius of organizing and public policy advocacy under such circumstances is not having created all the conditions for success, but rather recognizing when those conditions approach and taking advantage of them.

In our case, we continued to hold onto "our block" and to advance our cause. From a local policy perspective, we knew that once any one building on the block was torn down it was only a matter of time before the entire block fell. So we took a multi-faceted approach to preservation that entailed block clean-ups, block parties, the development of gardens, starting of a food cooperative, and other collective activities designed to both bring people together and to fight the prevailing sentiment that the area was beyond hope. We developed a position paper that defended our work at preserving and upgrading the block and called on the government and foundations to assist our efforts. We wrote proposals. We met with every local institution to explain our program and get their support. We participated at every local Community Board meeting and at every borough-level meeting concerning budget, land use and community development matters. We testified at local and citywide public hearings on the same topics. We sought the support of elected officials. We participated in task forces regarding the city's treatment of "abandoned" properties and how those properties should be redeveloped once the city had ownership. We did legal research, discovering laws that would allow the city to take over the privately-owned Kelly Street property even in the absence of an *in rem* tax foreclosure proceeding. Under a section (19A) of the New York State Real Property Actions and Proceedings Law the city could foreclose on a property that threatened the health and safety of local residents and others. We made that case, and after almost a year of advocacy, we had the agreement of an Assistant Commissioner to propose such an action. (A new local law made that action moot when the city's housing agency was given new powers pursuant to a new "quick vesting" law.)

Finally, in August of 1977, we took over those three Kelly Street buildings and began cleaning them out and doing interior gut demolition. Our intention then was to demonstrate to the city and anyone with resources that we were serious, as well as to (hopefully) embarrass the city into providing us with the resources we needed to renovate the properties. In short, we did everything within our power to make our program successful.

Success in the Bronx. We were not operating in a vacuum. Other groups in the Bronx and the city were engaged in similar activities. A kind of "trade association" for such groups was formed – the Association of Neighborhood Housing Developers (now called the Association for Neighborhood and Housing Development, Inc.) This group began to provide citywide advocacy for efforts such as ours. The media and academic circles started referring to these efforts as the "Sweat Equity Movement," or the "Neighborhood Housing Movement."

All of this shows what we did for ourselves, what others in similar circumstances did for themselves, and what we did for one another through collective action.

Other external factors pushed our efforts over the top. These factors came together fortuitously for us.

- The New York City Comptroller published a report on city auctions. The report showed that by and large, properties auctioned were further abused and eventually returned to city ownership in worse shape than before, through foreclosures at a later date. This report effectively put a halt to city auctions of foreclosed residential real estate.
- The city's fiscal crisis prompted numerous newspaper investigative accounts of what were referred to as "phantom bookkeeping" on the city's part. A typical report would refer to the city's practice of counting anticipated real estate tax receipts in successive budgets, borrowing against these anticipated receipts and spending the money for city operations. The problem was that hundreds of millions of dollars of these anticipated receipts were never collected. This prompted the city's legislature to pass a law that was sponsored by the chair of the City Council's Finance Committee. The intent of the law, according to him, was to force landlords to pay their taxes under threat of foreclosure. The so-called "quick-vesting" law allowed the city to foreclose after only one year of tax arrears, instead of three. This law inadvertently resulted in the city foreclosing on tens of thousands of units of housing in generally dilapidated conditions. This solved our problem of the privately owned building on Kelly Street. It also created a property management problem for HPD, and our organization was able to enter into a contract with the city to manage several of these newly vested city- owned buildings, further institutionalizing our effort. From this humble beginning, the group would go on to take ownership of and manage over 1000 units of housing.
- By October of 1977, we had just about finished cleaning out 940 Kelly Street and were about to begin working to demolish everything in the building that could not be salvaged. We had still not made any progress with the

city budget, and we were growing weary of working without adequate resources. It was in that month that President Jimmy Carter visited the South Bronx. And because his visit included the building on Washington Avenue that was the first sweat equity project of a group called the Peoples Development Corporation (PDC), "sweat equity" became legitimate and was even referred to for a while as the "President's Program." The PDC received the bulk of all largesse resulting directly from the visit. However, there was credibility for the program overall and we were able to pull together the resources (about $700,000) necessary to do our first project – the sweat equity rehabilitation of those three Kelly Street buildings.

In the end, Banana Kelly succeeded as much on account of the forces of circumstance as by having made any direct impact on public policy. However, these circumstances did result in a major change in public policy with respect to the "quick vesting" law. One unintended result of that became the creation of the second largest system of public housing in the country, and we were able to protect and then redevelop those *in rem* properties within our neighborhood.

In Rem *Policy*. After that heady initial experience, I continued to attempt to change government policy regarding housing circumstances and opportunities in the South Bronx and similar neighborhoods. *In rem* policy remained important to my continued work at Banana Kelly and then at my citywide work at the Parodneck Foundation. As referred to above, I was part of the first *in rem* task force in the mid-seventies known as the Task Force on City Owned Property. Its purpose was to develop innovative disposition programs to allow the city to meet its federal mandate to dispose of the properties taken as quickly as possible in return for the federal government's agreement to allow the city to use federal Community Development Block Grant (CDBG) funds for maintenance and operations of the *in rem* housing stock.

At the time the city had about three years' worth of CDBG funds unspent (about $300 million dollars),[78] but federal rules precluded the use of such funds for "maintenance of effort." So the city needed a waiver to use the funds for the maintenance and operation of the *in rem* stock, a waiver they received with the proviso that the city aggressively dispose of the properties as they were obtained.

Why the city held onto the funds in the first place is beyond me. However, Lisa Kaplan (a long- time Lower East Side resident, advocate and not-for-profit housing development professional) told me about a meeting she and other Lower East Side advocates had with Roger Starr – then Administrator of the Housing Development Administration (the predecessor to the City's current Department of Housing Preservation and Development, HPD). When asked why CDBG funds were not made available to them to advance their housing plans, Starr reportedly stated that to fund them would be the equivalent of the Israeli government funding the PLO. If that was, indeed, his view, then since at the time there were few development options in inner city areas *except* through not-for-profit community groups, it is no surprise that the money accumulated unspent throughout most of the Beame administration.

The task force was successful, and as a result the city engaged in an aggressive campaign to upgrade and dispose of properties to not-for-profit developers and tenants. The city needed to manage a massive problem, seeking out all those who would be of use. Those available consisted mostly of residents who were willing to become working members of cooperatives and not-for-profit organizations. Because the private, for-profit sector represented the source of the "in rem problem" to begin with, it was not until the mid-eighties that the city would begin to sell these properties to private owners through a program called the Private Ownership Management Program.

---

[78] This unforgivable hording of public funds was the subject for much organizing and advocacy. The "Pratt Coalition" which grew out of a conference by Pratt Center, along with citywide groups such as ANHD, U-HAB and the Model Cities Coalition, eventually became the NYC Housing and Development Coalition, and kept both pressure on the city as well as a spotlight on these funds to ensure their eventual and appropriate public use.

In 1985, Joan Allen and I co-authored a report that was published by the New York Urban Coalition, the "Give-a-Damn" group from the sixties. The purpose of this report and the ensuing discussions among legislators, the private sector, not-for-profit community groups and advocates was to review then-current *in rem* policy and see if it should be changed. The recommendations in the report were based on a city fiscal environment that was still strained and focused attention on a portion of *in rem* stock that appeared to represent an "irreducible minimum" number of buildings which the city could not hope to sell, even for one dollar. As such and based upon the low incomes of the buildings' residents, the report recommended that some portion of the *in rem* stock should remain as a new form of public housing.

These recommendations were not well received, and once the city re-entered the bond markets in or around 1987, the issue of not being able to invest in and subsequently dispose of the buildings became somewhat moot when the city announced a major housing initiative whereby funding was provided to rehabilitate and dispose of all of its properties to tenants, not-for-profit and for-profit owners. But the report and the ensuing advocacy efforts did have many beneficial benefits to neighborhoods with a preponderance of *in rem* housing, as well as to the tenants who resided in most of these properties. And the report was successful in that it continued dialogue among the actors in this field and maintained leadership connections vital to ongoing program development and operation.

The "Missing Middle." In 1991, the city was in the throes of a recession. Many advocates feared that just as the recession of mid-seventies had created *in rem* housing, the recession of 1991 would prompt the expeditious sale of the remaining stock. The concerns of advocates at that time centered on the adequate rehabilitation of the sold properties, the reluctance on the part of the city to continue to take buildings in tax arrears, and the long- term affordability to residents for whom this was indeed housing of the last resort. I soon became chair of the newly formulated Task Force on City Owned Property, later renamed the Task Force on City Owned and Distressed Property (to include private sector distressed properties). Over the next ten years, primarily supported by the Parodneck Foundation, the Task Force published two major reports, mostly based upon research in the field overseen by Dr. Susan Saegert of the CUNY Graduate Center. Six thousand *in rem* and formerly *in rem* households were interviewed, and many interesting findings were reported. In the *in rem* buildings sold to private, for-profit landlords in the eighties through the Private Ownership Management Program, there was a demographic "missing middle." When the demographics of those privately-owned buildings were compared to demographics in all other *in rem* buildings, the post-sale resident population was overrepresented by both very low income (mostly formerly homeless) and middle income residents. One possible explanation for the missing middle is that private landlords were encouraged to take "Section 8" tenants from the shelters (the lower demographic category) for some of their units. They were then allowed to take middle income families in their other units. This strongly suggests that many of the former tenants, who were "working poor," were displaced.

Tenant Coops a Success. Another finding was that after city ownership, tenant cooperatives provided the best quality housing. Housing quality and housing satisfaction were both highest where the tenants were organized, regardless of ownership type. The research also revealed that organized resident groups, and particularly cooperative housing groups, had the highest levels of "helping activities," what would now be termed "social capital."

As a result of this research, we were able to obtain further funding to advance our program, which focused on sales that allowed for resident control, increased vesting schedules and other recommendations. Our advocacy advanced to the Deputy Mayor level, where two Deputy Mayors were on opposite sides of the issue. In the end, our recommendations did not win out. However, whether or not our recommendations prevailed, our efforts did serve to maintain some balance to city programs overall that permitted a substantial amount of not-for-profit and tenant control of this valuable housing stock.

The Giuliani Approach. As a mayoral candidate, Rudolf Giuliani made it clear at the one and only mayoral debate held with then-Mayor David Dinkins that he favored a private sector approach to housing preservation and development. Subsequently, the Giuliani administration exhibited an extraordinarily limited public policy scope, mostly centered around security, workfare and, to a lesser extent, education.

Two years into his administration, the Mayor announced a new *in rem* program – the "Building Blocks" program. I had the chance to affect public policy, but this time I chose not to take an antagonistic route. Instead, I tried to advance the one part of the program that I viewed as most useful and important.

The new program had a "tax lien sale" component and a "third party transfer" component. The Tax Lien Sale Program targeted so-called "marginal" buildings that were viewed as having some market value. For these buildings, instead of foreclosing on the city's tax lien, the city instead sold its tax liens as a bundle of receivables to an investment company. The investment company used the sale of bonds to fund the purchase and then served as a trustee for the city and collection agency on the part of those who invested in the bonds.

The Third Party Transfer program targeted those buildings that were not viewed as having a market value. These buildings were to be foreclosed by the city, as before, but instead of taking title, the city immediately transferred the property to a newly created subsidiary of the Enterprise Foundation, the Neighborhood Restore Housing Development Fund Corporation. The task for this new corporation was to take title, execute property management and sales contracts with city-chosen for-profit and not-for-profit developers. These developers were expected to place the buildings in legal compliance and secure all necessary financing within one year so that they could take title, renovate the properties and operate them as private rentals.

The problem was that the city aggressively pursued the tax lien sales but was slow to implement the Third Party Transfer program. My colleagues and I at CATCH and the Parodneck Foundation began to work with the city to implement the Third Party Transfer Program. When the list of potential properties was published, we visited each and every building to determine whether or not the buildings could work out a plan to prevent foreclosure. We were able to do this with one multiple dwelling and one small home occupied by a senior homeowner – the first on a technicality, the second through our senior home improvement and refinancing program. We worked with other buildings as well, maintaining contact with the local city staff assigned to work with landlords and generally assisting in advancing the program.

Third Party Transfer. Since getting distressed buildings out of private hands was a major goal in our prior advocacy efforts, you may well ask why we were assisting the city in getting buildings off the foreclosure list. The reason was because we perceived, rightly or wrongly, that the Giuliani administration had little interest in the Third Party Transfer program, preferring instead the Tax Lien Program. Our fear was that the program would never get off the ground if the city could not succeed in removing some of the better buildings from the list. This was after what was effectively a nine-year moratorium on the city taking distressed, private sector properties away from delinquent landlords. It was our position that the Third Party Transfer program would be our last, best chance of reviving public intervention into distressed, private sector properties during the Giuliani administration. We viewed the successful implementation of this program as a priority.

It took two years from the publication of the initial list to the implementation of the program. In the first, pilot round, the mutual housing organization, CATCH, was among the groups chosen for the program. In addition to our extensive experience with privately owned distressed properties, we had worked with agency staff in helping get the new program off the ground. CATCH ended up redeveloping about 100 units in the first round.

Sue Them! In the second round, we received three buildings but declined on two of them because we believed that we were ill-equipped to handle Single Room Occupancy buildings (SROs). The Urban Homesteading Assistance Group, or "U-HAB," the not-for-profit that was designated sponsor of the largest block of buildings in that second round, used an alternative means of advocacy to gain sponsorship of buildings. Consistent with their overall corporate mission, the group assisted residents of many of the targeted second round buildings in preparing a lawsuit against the city, claiming that the residents were denied the equal opportunities of the profit and not-for-profit companies to own their own buildings. The strategy worked, and a substantial number of buildings were given the opportunity to become cooperatives. Furthermore, public policy changes were made to provide residents with what amounted to a "right of first refusal" if these organized resident groups found legitimate not-for-profits to sponsor them. This meant that an organized group of residents could petition for cooperative ownership and prevail over any other applicant for the property.

As successful as the strategy was, however, the re-development has been more difficult. Just because people want to own their own buildings does not mean that they should or can. Training residents for cooperative housing is actually harder than training households for more conventional homeownership since there is the added complication of appreciating group capacities and working through group dynamics.

The lesson here is that lawsuits can never be rejected as a strategy. However, such a strategy must be taken with great forethought and consideration.

The 1975 NYC Charter Revision. Public policy formation through basic government revision can be examined through two recent charter revisions in New York City. Such charter revisions change the rules of the game, shuffle or change the players, and provide a new framework for the development and implementation of public policy.

Under the New York City Charter adopted in the mid-seventies, the prior basic framework of governance was held intact, with some minor, though useful, revisions. Among the most important are the following:

1. No city land could be sold or leased without having gone through a land use review process known as the Uniform Land Use Review Process, or ULURP. (Initially, it was recommended that this local review process be called the *Standard* Land Use Review Procedure, until someone noticed that the acronym would be "SLURP"!)

2. Community Boards, a rather informal structure of local review groups started in the sixties, were institutionalized, staffed, and provided with a role in land use, budgeting, zoning, and other matters. Consonant with the formalization of 59 Community Boards each overseeing districts with approximately 100,000 people, it was mandated that where possible city services be organized in a "co-terminus" manner, meaning that city services "districts" have the same boundaries as community boards.
3. The "master planning" requirement in the prior city charter was eliminated in favor of a new section 197-a, which allowed for official city plans that were to be developed by the community boards themselves, among others.

All in all, the mid-seventies New York City Charter revision was a "good government" coup and what many saw as the beginning of a process of decentralized government that would evolve to provide more power locally. Overall, the basic governance of New York City remained the same. The City Council retained 35 members (still called "Councilmen") and continued as the city's legislative body, although the body was often mocked as having little more than the power to name streets. The Mayor continued as the Chief Executive of the city, overseeing all city agencies and the expenditure of all city funds. The Comptroller oversaw the registration of all city contracts, the city's bonding process, and had audit authority over all agencies. The City Council President "presided" over the Council, but only had a vote in the case of a tie.

The real power of the various offices came with the votes on the Board of Estimate. The Borough Presidents were, theoretically, the "chief executives" of their respective boroughs, and sat on the Board of Estimate, a carryover from the creation of New York City from the cities of New York and Brooklyn and the counties of the Bronx, Queens, and Richmond. But in reality, the Borough Presidents' power came from their ability to stop or slow down proposed mayoral actions.

The Board of Estimate was comprised of eight members. Three citywide officials (the Mayor, City Council President, and Comptroller) each had two votes. The Borough Presidents each had one vote. So on matters of import, such as the adoption of a new zoning resolution, approval of major (and countless numbers of routine) land use development projects, approval of every city contract of more than a certain amount of money or with a term in excess of one year, approval of the city budget and other important matters, the Mayor was forced to work with other members of the Board of Estimate. This forced the Mayor to justify his actions and made government about as transparent as it can get. It also allowed groups and individuals to make a case for or against a project to eight different political entities.

Every City Council President I have known always had one eye on the mayoralty, so any opportunity to exhibit leadership on an issue in opposition to the Mayor became a potential platform for higher office. This became an avenue for democratic redress for citizens seeking a "hero."

The borough presidents would very often vote in a block to maximize their effectiveness. In those cases, all they needed was the vote of one citywide official to prevail. Or, if the other two citywide officials and two borough presidents voted in a block, they would prevail. And as a courtesy extended to all of the representatives on the board of estimate, any city wide- official and any borough president (on matters affecting his or her borough) could table any item for at least one month, to the next meeting. Needless to say, this provided for a wide range of advocacy approaches and organizing strategies.

The process could be cumbersome, but it allowed for a great deal of citizen and group input and provided many opportunities for effective citizen intervention to affect an outcome.

The 1989 Charter Revision. The impetus behind the 1989 charter revision was a lawsuit brought on the constitutional basis of "one person, one vote." The primary legal point of the lawsuit is best made through considering the Brooklyn Borough President, who had one vote on the Board of Estimate, and the Staten Island Borough President also had one vote, even though his borough had only one person for every ten Brooklyn inhabitants. However, a lawsuit premised on violating the rights of citizens resulted in a city government that was less transparent, more centralized, and less accountable.

Interestingly, the original formation of New York City is analogous to the formation of this country. The fact that the United States Senate violates the same constitutional requirement is a testament to the fact that the union of states was based on political compromise, which included a legislative body that treated each of the states as equal, regardless of population. But where the federal government is exempt from this proscription, localities were not.

So New York City established a new Charter Revision Commission, chaired by former New York City Corporation Counsel, Frederick Schwartz (part of the F.A.O. Schwartz family).

Citizens for Charter Change. There were many ways to fix this constitutional deficiency, and a group quickly formed to provide organized citizen and group input into the process. The group's leadership was comprised of Manhattan Borough President Ruth Messinger, Congressman Major Owens, and numerous labor leaders. The group was called Citizens for Charter Change (CCC), and I joined up early on, as did many other representatives of citywide advocacy groups and community development organizations. In all, there were about 30 or more active CCC members. As the Commission staffed up and began its public process of preparing drafts and soliciting public comment, the Citizens for Charter Change developed a parallel process of analyzing proposals, getting them out to various constituency groups and then organizing formal and informal responses to the Charter Revision Commission.

As proposals began to take shape, many of us on the CCC committee developed serious reservations, and some very heated discussions took place among this subset of community and advocacy leaders. It was clear that this group was not going to hold together without extraordinary leadership if it chose to take on the Commission head on and work to defeat the proposed charter revision at the next November election.

Objections Raised. As opposed to weighing the vote of borough presidents based on population, the commission was recommending abolishing the Board of Estimate in favor of a more powerful mayor and a City Council with greater powers. Many of us predicted that this charter revision recommendation would create an "imperial mayor," make cheerleaders out of the borough presidents, and create an ineffective legislative body.

At one point, Ruth Messinger and a small leadership group had a private meeting with Fritz Schwartz. To this day, I have no idea what transpired at that meeting or who in fact attended, but shortly thereafter Messinger took positions in line with the recommendations of the Commission. When it became clear that the Citizens for Charter Change was going to endorse the recommendations, a number of us broke off from the group and began to work on defeating the revision proposal at the ballot.

The reasons set forth by the Citizens for Charter Change group for the support of the Commission's proposals were varied. They included certain concessions agreed to by the Commission, such as the hiring of planners and the city funding of Environmental Impact Statements. (These concessions are discussed in Chapter 6 of this book, along with the realities of these supposed victories.)

At any rate, for the next year or two, a group of us toured the city, at first fighting for defeat of the charter revision proposal as it was to appear on the ballot. At most public meetings, on cable programs and in print, you would hear or read about many people speaking against the proposal, among them: Bronx Borough President Fernando Ferrer, Sam Sue and Eddie Bautista of New York Lawyers for the Public Interest, Marcy Benstock of the Clean Air Campaign, Bonnie Brower of ANHD, Marie Dormuth of Chelsea, leaders of numerous Queens Civic Associations, such as Pat Dolan, and myself.

By election day, it was clear that we would face defeat. The Commission mounted a very well-financed and effective educational and outreach campaign. Furthermore, a strong Mayor was exactly what the business sector of the city wanted because it was believed that a strong and centralized executive branch of city government could best facilitate the development needs of an international city and world financial center. Finally, the liberal political community in New York City was split, and many never bothered to participate in the process or learn what the proposals actually said. The Charter Revision was passed in November of 1989.

Rulemaking. Did my group sit around crying into our beers? No: we then worked nearly as hard as city staff on the all-important rulemaking process that followed the Charter Revision adoption. We were quite successful in the rulemaking process, due to our persistence and our willingness to go the extra mile, including complete alternative rewrites of the so-called "Fair Share" rules and substantial editing of other new rules.

Even though the potential for an "imperial mayoralty" was lost on David Dinkins, who was too nice a man to arrogate so much power to himself, it was not lost on Rudy Giuliani. He knew how to use the very substantial power of his office, and he did so throughout his eight years as mayor. Time will tell whether the City Council will ever become an effective countervailing political force to the Mayor. But even if it does, New York City is no longer as transparent as it once was, and citizens and groups have greatly lessened access to government than they had under the previous charter.

Welfare Reform. Before I leave the topic of policy, I would like to at least touch on the issue of welfare reform. As President, Bill Clinton promised to "end welfare as we know it," and he was true to his word. George W. Bush is not as focused on the issue, except that every dollar of entitlement and discretionary funds targeted to the poor in the federal budget is under attack in favor of increased support for the military and tax cuts.

When it comes to welfare and treatment of the poor in general, this country is hypocritical in the extreme. From Ronald Reagan's "welfare queens" using food stamps to buy vodka, to pseudo-journalists and commentators of the current day claiming that federal rental subsidies motivate women to flock to homeless shelters,[79] age-old notions of the "undeserving poor" have found new currency in the modern day welfare reform debate. Now, once again, after a brief liberal period in which poverty was mistakenly viewed as pathology, sus-

---

[79] See almost any issue of City Journal, published by the far-right Manhattan Institute, whose writers for the most part write editorials in the guise of journalism. Reference to the rental subsidy position is from "The Housing Reform That Backfired," by Howard Husock, *City Journal*, Summer 2004.

ceptible to cure through random social services, minimal public support, and some improvements in education, we are once again blaming the poor for their own circumstances. Now, poverty is no longer viewed as pathology but as a matter of personal choice, even preference. With this assumption prevailing, punishment through denial of basic needs and denial of freedom is now seen as the cure – not to the individual's circumstances but to society's burden of having to tolerate them.

As a resident of the South Bronx for over two decades, I have been known many people who survived on welfare and other forms of public assistance. Furthermore, I have lived in poverty myself, by choice – not because I wanted to be poor but because I wanted to pursue community development work. While organizing Banana Kelly, there was a stretch of time when I had no income at all. (Admittedly, this situation only lasted a few months.) When I became the first Executive Director of Banana Kelly in 1978, my initial salary was $13,000 – approximately $39,000 today. When I left to pursue a job with the Parodneck Foundation in 1982 at age 29, my starting salary was $25,000 – about $50,000 today). At the time that I met my wife, now a successful real estate professional, Helena was herself on welfare, raising her three children on her own.

So I know about welfare, and certainly it can be a terrible thing. In my opinion it does breed dependency in many people, as well as motivating others to self-destructive and/or anti-social behavior. But to take that reality as conclusive and dispositive of the entire matter is simply wrong.

Welfare is designed to provide subsistence to the indigent sufficient to allow other, more privileged members of society, to benefit more than they otherwise would be able to if the political system was more equitable. If this country was truly committed to welfare reform, then programs would be developed that have the following components:

1. Only the disabled would be provided welfare as an entitlement and only to the extent of their disability.

2. All other able-bodied persons would be required to work (and to the extent possible, disabled persons would be required as well) – BUT ALL WOULD BE PAID A REAL LIVING WAGE.
3. To the extent that sufficient private sector jobs were unavailable, public works programs would be created.
4. Universal child and health care would be the norm, with child care extending to after school programs to ensure that children are supervised and provided with productive outlets while parents worked.
5. Those who refused to work would not receive any but the most meager public benefits.

Such a program would accomplish two ends simultaneously, things that would scare to death any "conservative" concerned with personal responsibility (responsibility to themselves, that is).

1. It would debunk the myth of the lazy poor.
2. It would require a system that would of necessity preclude excessive compensation and wealth accumulation, whether this applies to Michael Jordan or to Michael Eisner.

The Importance of Public Policy for Community Developers. In conclusion, it is important for community development groups to understand the importance of public policy in undertaking their activities. Public policy often provides the resources to accomplish these activities. Public policy provides the formal processes required for approval or acquiescence of such activities and the rules by which the programs developed pursuant to public policies are carried out. Also, public policy provides for the authority of the public sector (or private sector forces) to frustrate or altogether foreclose opportunities which serve a group's community interest. This is why involvement in public policy matters is a critical component of community development work. With collective effort, strategic planning and a bit of luck, policy change is possible.

XIII The Importance of Place

> People seek out places where they feel competent and confident, places where they can make sense of the environment while also being engaged with it.[80]

If I were entering college now, I would consider majoring in environmental psychology. This new interdisciplinary field has particular relevance to community development. The importance of "place" is explained in environmental psychology as "place attachment" and "place identity." These very real connections need to be appreciated, understood, and accommodated in our community development work, whether that work involves preservation, renovation, or new development.

When I first returned to New York City in 1971 as a student at Manhattan College, I was exhilarated by the rich diversity of people and the fact that there were so many different identifiable neighborhoods. Most people are familiar with New York's famous neighborhoods, such as Chinatown or Little Italy, but not everybody knows that there are geographical neighborhoods with constantly changing ethnic compositions scattered throughout every corner of the city.

In the South Bronx alone, I became very familiar with the Hunts Point, Longwood, Mott Haven, Morrisania, Highbridge, Tremont, and Morris Heights

---

[80] R. DeYoung, "Environmental Psychology," D.E. Alexander and R.W. Fairbridge, Eds., *Encyclopedia of Environmental Science*, Kluwer, 1999. .

neighborhoods. And when I began to work and live in the Hunts-Point/ Longwood neighborhood, I learned how there were notable differences from one block to the next. The block I began organizing on in 1976 was known as "Banana Kelly" because of its curve. The block just south of it was referred to as "Straight Kelly," a block that was mostly demolished through urban renewal programs just prior to the public housing moratorium of 1973. (Today, "Straight Kelly" is gone, replaced by the Bill Rainey Park.) And the block just south of that was known as "Country Kelly," because of its neat rows of semi-attached brownstones.

Place Attachment. These affectionate designations testify to the fact that the people who lived in the South Bronx were attached to it, even though it was in terrible shape. In the seventies, the South Bronx had the highest unsolved homicide rate in the nation, along with a slew of other negative social indicators: high rates of welfare, teenage pregnancy, high school drop-outs, etc. Nonetheless, many of the area residents seemed attached to their neighborhoods – at least until the onslaught of the fires in the mid-seventies.

Throughout my decades as a community development organizer in the South Bronx, I was often amazed at how protective people were within a one-block area. No matter what went on beyond it, the block was sanctuary – at least for those who had social supports on that block, such as extended families and friends.

Once, a teenager visiting someone on Intervale Avenue got into a scuffle with some gang members there. He managed to flee, but he heard that members of the Savage Skulls were going to come looking for him that night on his block. When he told his story, the block organized a defense. Scores of residents went to the rooftops with bricks in hand. When the Savage Skulls entered the block they were pummeled with bricks from both sides of the street. They were never able to carry out their threat, and they never returned.

Pride in the South Bronx, which was home to over 600,000 people, seemed to dissolve when the fires began in earnest. I often heard young people say that only losers would stay in the area: the only way for a young person to succeed was to leave. One small child told me that the South Bronx had nothing to be proud of except for the Bronx Zoo. When the physical devastation of the seventies turned into the social plague of the eighties (the crack epidemic and all that went with it), I was not terribly surprised. The violence and outright disregard for life that accompanied the crack epidemic was occurring amid utter physical devastation. The human habitat had been destroyed.

Social Design. Environmental psychology is especially pertinent to three areas of community development: design, program development, and program evaluation.

Architectural and urban planning work is often viewed as a strictly professional undertaking, detached from the concerns and activities of ordinary humans. Often, this form of detached design work is more concerned with spatial opportunities and constraints, regulatory requirements, engineering possibilities and artistic ingenuity than with the transformation of space into usable living or working areas for particular populations of people.

In the early 1980s, one of the early pioneers of environmental psychology, Robert Somner, coined or adopted the phrase "social design"[81] to refer to design work that entailed:

> …working with people rather than for them; involving people in the planning and management of the spaces around them…educating them…[to] achieve a harmonious balance between the social, physical, and natural environment…

A primary goal of social design is to create physical settings that accommodate those who are going to use the spaces. As obvious as this goal may seem, too often design work is done in a vacuum of "objective" standards, financial constraints, and assumed values. Consider, for example, the design of senior residential facilities. In many facilities, designers have simply assumed that "congregate facilities" within the housing accommodations should be maximized. However, surveys of residents show that seniors place a premium on

---

[81] Robert Gifford, *Environmental Psychology, Principles & Practices*, Allyn & Bacon, 1997, p. 381.

privacy and desire social opportunities on a much more limited basis than is generally assumed.

Untested Assumptions. I had a similar personal experience with untested assumptions as a group worker for the Casita Maria Settlement House in the early seventies. I saw that our center never planned any outings for the seniors, so I began to work with the director of the program to plan some trips. It took me several meetings with the director of the senior center to realize that the seniors wanted nothing more than lunch and bingo and then home – probably in time to catch the afternoon *novelas*. They were perfectly content with this arrangement and had no interest in my museum outings.

Goals of Social Design. In the field of industrial design, "scientific management" techniques date back to the nineteenth century. Intensive studies were performed about how to design factories to obtain the greatest human productivity possible, and the results of these studies were widely applied. Careful, integrative design can go a long way towards modifying behavior and environmental psychology takes scientific management of space to a new (and non-exploitative) level. As an example, studies have shown that allowing institutionalized patients to participate in planning their own spaces cuts down violent behavior. This is consistent with other research that shows a direct relationship between lack of control over personal space and increased levels of stress.

So another goal of social design is to enhance the sense of personal control the anticipated occupant will have over the developed space. People need to feel a connection to, and have some sense of control over, their environments. Indeed, such a relationship between an individual and his or her environment is viewed as a critical basis for a person feeling good about him or herself and productively interacting with others.

Another goal of social design is to create spaces that encourage "helping activities." Helping activities are those activities that make for what is commonly viewed as "neighborliness." Of late, the manifestation of such activities has been described as "social capital." These activities include watching younger children when a mother needs to go to the market; helping a senior resident with her weekly shopping requirements; giving advice; watching someone's laundry as they leave the laundry room to perform other chores, and so on.

Design can promote or hinder such helping activities. Interestingly, not only design but also the form of ownership facilitates "helping activities." In the mid-nineties I chaired a citywide advocacy group named the Task Force on City Owned and Distressed Property. We commissioned Dr. Susan Saegert of the Housing Environments Research Group of the CUNY Graduate School to oversee a survey of over 6,000 units of housing that was either in city ownership (*in rem*) or was formerly in city ownership. This was and remains as of this writing, the largest such survey ever conducted for *in rem* and formerly *in rem* buildings. Among the many findings was that the low-income cooperatives that were developed through the city's *in rem* programs had the greatest incidences of helping activities. An even more important finding was that, regardless of ownership, the incidence of helping activities within buildings was directly correlated to the level of social organization within the building. In other words, tenant cooperatives had the most "social capital" at work within their buildings, but even private, for-profit buildings with active tenant associations had substantial amounts of helping activities going on.[82]

Defensible Space. Public housing projects are notoriously lacking in design characteristics that promote neighborliness. That is because they were built for efficiency: the primary concern was the number of human beings that could safely and comfortably fit into the available space. Public housing is designed as though human beings are individual, self-contained social units without social needs. The "towers on the parks" projects, such as most of the public housing projects built during the urban renewal period (1949 to 1973), were designed to optimize residential space and then provide compensatory "green" space surrounding the towers. But the open areas soon became dangerous since

---

[82] See two reports published by the Parodneck Foundation: *Housing in the Balance*, 1993, Op. cit. and *No More Housing of the Last Resort*, by Michele Cotton, with Prof. Susan Saegert and David Reiss, 1995.

they were totally segregated from the majority of housing units. Furthermore, they were void of legal commercial activities and had no relation to the normal scale of human interaction. Where there is no commercial development and the green space is simply used to get to and from a destination, it doesn't get used for the kind of activity for which it was designed: namely, passive family and active youth recreation. Urban parks within projects are not seen as defensible space.

Defensible space is that which "increases the residents' sense of ownership, eliminates space about which no one feels vigilant, and increases space that is easily watched by residents."[83] This area of environmental psychology owes much to Jane Jacobs, since so much of her seminal work describes how defensible space is achieved through the normal operations of a viable, mixed-use, and diverse neighborhood, without the need for retaining walls, gated communities, or private security forces.

Intuitive Design. Another goal of social design is to ensure that whatever "place" is developed allows for a minimum of confusion and facilitates easy maneuverability, so people find their way intuitively, without getting lost or confused. The best-known example of intuitive design is Grand Central Station, where thousands of newcomers each day manage to cross the vast spaces without much need for direction. In community development, examples of social design would be the placement of children's play areas in full view of parents inside a house or apartment or beside adults who are a part of the fabric of a neighborhood activity, such as shopkeepers and resident adults coming and going. Social design in interior home lay-outs allow for circulation that matches how people live: bathrooms placed near bedrooms and home offices that do not adjoin the living areas. We expect that designers of commercial strips will place them along the main course of pedestrian and vehicular traffic.

Such predictability is important to us in our daily lives.

---

[83] Gifford, R. Op. cit., p.137.

One reason we work so hard to keep our surroundings predicable is that we rely on them to help us segue smoothly from role to role throughout the day.[84]

Even designing a residence so that toddlers can look out the windows has been shown to enhance the early cognitive development of children.[85]

Healthy social development is also advanced by a safe and nurturing environment. Perhaps astonishingly,

> Studies of juvenile delinquency and high school drop-outs rates, for example, demonstrate that a child is better off in a good neighborhood and a troubled family than he or she is in a troubled neighborhood and a good family. Children are powerfully shaped by their external environment, [and] the features of our immediate social and physical world – the streets we walk down, the people we encounter – play a huge role in shaping who we are and how we act.[86]

Sometimes it seems like community or city planners have deliberately tried to confuse and frustrate people. Take a ride some day along Central Avenue from Yonkers to Scarsdale. Turn off the Avenue and down any street and you will probably find yourself in a virtual maze of streets that were seemingly designed to punish you for venturing beyond the commercial strip and into the residential area. Once you make the mistake of turning down a side street, you might assume that by making a turn in one direction or another you could get back to Central Avenue. But no: instead the road winds in another direction. Now one might say that Greenwich Village is somewhat the same. However, Greenwich Village has an excuse: its streets were patterned after former cow paths!

Architects Who Listen. There are different phases to any good social design process. These include an analysis of the design goals, an understanding of the client's perceived and actual needs, and an assessment of the fiscal or physical constraints upon the project. This leads to the actual design in the "synthesis

---

[84] Winifred Gallagher, *The Power of Place*, Harper Collins, 1993, p.129.
[85] Gifford, R. Op. cit., p. 212, referring to the work of A.W. Gottfried and A.E. Gottfried.
[86] Gladwell, M. Op. cit., pp. 167-168.

stage," where all the desires, expressed needs, as well as contradictions, are played out within the context and confines of the planned development.

Over the years, I have had the good fortune to work with excellent architects who make it a practice to be social designers. For the most part, they have enjoyed working with the clients – mainly the residents of the buildings being redeveloped. The best architects are good listeners who know how to reconcile conflicting goals and place a technical frame on the ideas of the client group. With a little help, most tenants can arrive at what they actually want and need. Good social designers can work through any confusion to a practicable outcome. Of course, this technique goes beyond building and apartment design. I have seen it work in the development of urban renewal plans, the creation of new traffic patterns, and the design of parks.

People who live in an area know the area. They know the places to avoid. They know the patterns of pedestrian, truck, school-bound children, and other forms of traffic. I have often heard residents voice some concern or a practical way to make something work to a professional with a social design perspective. The designer or architect then translates that common-sense concern or solution into professional language and a planning rationale.

Program Development. Moving beyond design, the second use of environmental psychology in community development is in program development.

In planning efforts regarding housing, density considerations are often taken into account. One of New York City's most successful low-income housing programs is a tax credit plan called the Neighborhood Redevelopment Program. Among its many goals is the lessening of density in apartments. Where there is a grown child with her own children living with her parent, an attempt is made to provide her with her own apartment. Much evidence supports the conclusion that high density leads to psychological stress.

However, low density is not always a good thing! Very low density can lead to a loss of social support and concomitant psychological stress. Some environmental psychologists such as J. L Freedman even believe that density is not

The Concept of Community

a problem in and of itself. Density is neutral; it merely magnifies whatever else is going on.

> It is the task of social scientists is to specify the conditions under which high density leads to happy and unhappy outcomes.[87]

Overcrowding. As someone who has developed low income housing for nearly 30 years, I believe that density is an important design consideration. Overcrowding leads to added stress in households where there is already stress, and it is the exceptional household that exists stress-free. Stress is especially prevalent in low income households where money is tight, life's options are limited, and cumulative strains compound the discomfort of overcrowding. It may be true, as Gifford suggests, that

> Under high density conditions if we are able to attain one or more of these forms of control [cognitive, behavioral, or decisional], crowding stress will be reduced.[88]

But to attain such controls is often impossible when domestic stress is compounded by stress which is economic (work-related), social (extended family) and physiological (health problems such as asthma).

Besides the social aspects of high density household formations, overcrowding also leads to strains on the housing systems, such as plumbing, entrance doors, intercom, and elevators. Overcrowding is also an important consideration in the maintenance and operating budgets of low income housing.

Disasters. Environmental psychology also affects program development when the program is in response to a disaster, be it natural, or man-made. I have often speculated that the intensity of the crack epidemic in the late 1980s and early 1990s affecting the South Bronx and other inner city areas bore a direct relation to the severity of the physical devastation of these areas in the 1970s. I

---

[87] Gifford, R. Op. cit., p. 164, referring to a J.L. Freedman article in the *Psychological Review*, 1979.
[88] *Ibid*, pp. 65-166, referring to the work of Donald Schmidt and John Keating.

have lived through numerous drug fads, from heroin, to angel dust, free-based cocaine, crack-cocaine, methamphetamine ("Crystal Meth") and ecstasy. I have never seen anything as bad as what occurred at the street level with the selling and use of crack.

In the early nineties, a gang of young residents held our entire block hostage. The allure of crack was that it was cheap. Crack additives varied the high and allowed for different, marketed brands of crack on different blocks. On our block, "DOA," "TKO" and "Bad Boy" were the crack brands (referred to as "crack stamps") sold at that time. Other blocks had different brands.

My family had moved from Banana Kelly to "Country Kelly" in 1982. At the time, the block was reeling from the effects of arson and abandonment that plagued most of the area. The Longwood Historic District Community Association was struggling to implement an excellent preservation plan. But in spite of their efforts and our participation with the group, there was never the kind of social cohesion that existed on Banana Kelly – just two blocks away!

It was tragic to see an entire generation of young people destroy themselves, either through drug abuse, or through drug selling, which resulted in the dealers' eventual death or incarceration. Furthermore, young girls gravitated toward the street dealers, who had cash, cars, and drugs. Eventually these girls got pregnant and left school. They were ultimately abandoned, left alone to raise their children, some of whom were "crack babies," leading to further problems. On my block on Kelly Street in the late eighties and early nineties, at one time or another most of the youth on the block were involved in selling crack, running guns, serving as look-outs or assisting in making other supportive arrangements for the crack trade.

In the chapter entitled "Family Systems and Deurbanization: Implications for Substance Abuse," Wallace, Fullilove and Wallace maintain that the devastation that occurred in the seventies was of such a scale as to cause the "collective stress" that results in pervasive and sustained anti-social and deviant behavior.

> A considerable amount of literature suggests that the great outbreak of contagious urban decay and associated mass migration that has particularly devastated the

minority communities of New York City since the 1970s… will have a great and lasting impact on the occurrence of a broad spectrum of individual and collective deviant and other behaviors – behaviors that are profoundly implicated in population health status and, particularly, patterns of substance use and abuse.[89]

A similar point is made by Rodrick and Deborah Wallace when they state that the

criminology literature describes a vicious circle of community physical destruction leading to social disintegration, causing violent and deviant behaviors.[90]

There may even be some relation between the "collective stress" caused by violent urban devastation and the psychological condition of attachment disorder, whereby those who are removed from supportive, nurturing and loving families at an early age, grow up without any ability to empathize, and sympathize. These people often become abusive – sometime even murderous. Perhaps what occurred in the South Bronx and similar areas in the seventies and early eighties resulted in a form of massive attachment disorder, ultimately manifested in a total disregard for one's self and others.

How do we plan and implement community development programs to deal with the problems of such disasters?

If there is an earthquake or famine, we understand that these are disasters born of nature, beyond anyone's control, and we help the victims. Similarly, when the World Trade Center towers was struck by terrorists, killing almost three thousand people and directly affecting tens of thousands more, we did not blame the victims. In fact, we contributed unprecedented amounts of charitable funds to compensate their families.

But when the Bronx burned, directly affecting hundreds of thousands of people, our "programmatic" responses were not so charitable. Many did blame

---

[89] J. Lowinson et al, eds., *Comprehensive Textbook of Substance Abuse*, Williams and Wilkins, 1992, p. 948.
[90] Rodrick Wallace and Deborah Wallace, "The Coming Crisis of Public Health in the Suburbs," *The Milbank Quarterly*, Vol. 71, No. 4, 1993.

the victims. Even now, many people believe that the people who lived in the South Bronx and other inner city areas across the nation actually burned their own homes (although, as we have seen, the widespread arson was mainly caused by landlord agents). Such conclusions allow us to detach, and detachment allows us to decline assistance or even consider the need for such assistance.

As the seventies rolled into the eighties, New York City regained some of its fiscal integrity, and the inner city areas began to receive help in the form of housing investment. However, this help was not comprehensive, and it lacked integration. In that period, vacant lots were transformed into sites for small homes, and vacant buildings were renovated, many exclusively for homeless families. Very little was done based on any inclusive local discussions or as part of a comprehensive neighborhood-wide planning initiative. So for many of those who survived the devastation, this "re-investment" in their neighborhood must have seemed something not intended for their benefit, further compounding their isolation, frustration and helplessness.

Formula for Distress. In his textbook, Gifford offers a formula which gives mathematical expression to the concept of individual distress.[91]

$$\text{Distress} = \frac{\text{Exposure to Stressors} + \text{Vulnerability}}{\text{Psychological resources} + \text{Social Resources}}$$

According to this formulation, "exposure to stress" and individual "vulnerability" are mitigated and possibly even eliminated by the individual's "psychological resources" and the available "social resources." What if social resources are non-existent? This leaves people with only their own psychological resources, which would necessarily adapt to survive in conditions of explosive destruction and out-migration. Under these circumstances, it is understandable that the way to adapt and survive is to become insensitive to property rights, to civil rights, and even to basic human rights. Viewing the conditions this way,

---

[91] Gifford, R. Op. cit., p.337.

we can see why the adaptation took the form of increased gang activity (self-generated social resources), drug activity (me first, since no one else cares), and violence (diminished regard for human and property rights).

Programmatic Response. If the government were to design an intervention strategy, one would think it would create programs to enhance social resources. Instead, in the eighties and early nineties the city re-developed many inner city areas by focusing investment on those who could survive without having to rely on direct public assistance. The new neighborhood residents were installed within perimeter-fenced properties and were able to drive their kids to private school, shop outside the area, and generally live apart from the "other neighborhood" still suffering from the effects of the prior decade's violent destruction.

In the latter part of the seventies, New York City had one dominant housing program – demolition. If a vacant building did not have a federal set-aside commitment for Section 8 funds, the building was on a demolition list. As we entered the eighties, the city focused its housing programs in two areas – renovation and sale of *in rem* properties, and development of small homes on vacant lots. This program benefited many areas but was not part of any comprehensive plan. So the development of vacant land for perimeter-fenced one and two-family homes affronted those surviving residents of the South Bronx who were not housed there. Each unit of fenced housing said to those outside the fence, "THIS is not for you!"

Many of the low income buildings that survived landlord abandonment and eventually became tenant-sponsored cooperatives, developed siege mentalities, for understandable reasons. One building, 865 East 167th Street became known as "The Fortress" for this very reason. All of the residents looked out for one another. Strangers were not welcome. Applicants for apartments were tightly screened for appropriateness (which likely included ethnic background). Social stress and seemingly indiscriminate (or discriminating) redevelopment creates new categories of "haves" and "have-nots." If you have yours, protect it from your neighbors. If you are not among the chosen few, then take what you can, "and the devil take the hindmost."

By the mid-eighties, "the block" was no longer a harbor of safety, attachment and identity for its residents. While I could organize in the seventies beginning with the social networks that operated at street level and were obvious to anyone who spent time on the block, by the nineties, it became nearly impossible to organize in that way. To this day, many residents will not even meet in lobbies with neighbors whom they suspect of having children in the drug trade (even though drug activity across the board is much less than it had been). Today, most of our organizing work begins in the apartments of tenants and it expands slowly from there.

Program Evaluation. Program evaluation is another area in which environmental psychology assists the field of community development. Any planning process, whether a community initiative or the redesign of a single residential building, should include some evaluation after completion to see if the programmatic assumptions behind the design actually work in reality. Even though such a concluding exercise is reasonable and responsible, it is often ignored.

The Concept of Entopia. Toward the end of Gifford's textbook on environmental psychology, he distinguishes the work of environmental psychologists from classical philosophers. First he analyses the word "utopia," referring to the Greek words *eutopia*, "good place," and *outopia*, "no place," as forming the basis of Sir Thomas Moore's "utopia" as a good place beyond realization. Then he concludes,

> Utopia is not what we environmental psychologists aim for. We have a different topia in mind: entopia, which roughly means "achievable place."[92]

As today's community planners try to create entopia, their efforts are enriched by insights from the new field of environmental psychology.

---

[92] Gifford, R. Op. cit., p. 412.

The Concept of Community

XIV Banana Kelly Revisited

2007 was the year that Banana Kelly restored its reputation and its capacity, preserving its legacy for generations to come. Banana Kelly had known some rough times.

In the summer of 2002, I received a phone call from a long time associate, Marla Simpson. At the time, Marla was working for the New York State Attorney General Elliot Spitzer (now New York State Governor). She was wrapping up a two-year investigation looking into corruption and mismanagement at Banana Kelly Community Improvement Association, Inc. I hadn't worked for the organization for 17 years.

Initially (in the mid-seventies), the staffing and residency patterns of the early Banana Kelly organization were relatively balanced. Once the organization was established, however, a new struggle arose. Banana Kelly essentially began as a block association. But by 1981, it had grown to a mature CDC, with an array of development, property management, energy conservation, employment and other programs in operation. And the reach of the organization now extended well beyond the block, covering the entire Hunts-Point/Longwood area.

It became apparent to me that, as a membership organization, Banana Kelly needed to restructure its governance to include representation for and by the "new" members of the organization. But the discussion always broke down at the board level, with board members taking the position that "they" (the new members) do not need to have a role in governance; "we will speak for them."

It was at about this time that I left the organization and not long afterwards that the organization started its downward spiral.

In 2002, Banana Kelly was laboring under defaults, debarments, foreclosures, bankruptcy, and mountains of debt. The organization had been barred from city and state contracting. As it was unable to provide audited financial statements, its grant funding dried up. The Local Initiative Support Corporation and the Enterprise Foundation, both national intermediaries connecting tax credit investors with not-for-profit low-income housing developers, removed nearly half of Banana Kelly's portfolio, about 420 units, from the organization's control. The FBI was in the middle of an investigation. The Internal Revenue Service and State of New York were each owed upwards of $1 million in unpaid withholding taxes. The New York State Insurance Fund was owed hundreds of thousands of dollars for unpaid workers compensation charges. And the buildings themselves were in shocking disrepair.

Marla Simpson asked me to review a draft legal complaint and to consider becoming a member of a newly constituted board of directors once the Attorney General's office succeeded in forcing the removal of Banana Kelly's leadership. A last-minute deal was struck, and the Banana Kelly leadership, headed by Yolanda Rivera, voluntarily agreed to relinquish control. I agreed to be part of the board, and I helped recruit other board members.

Ferrer on Board. In November of 2002, our new board was formally installed. At that first board meeting, Fernando Ferrer, the former Bronx Borough President, was elected chairman. I was elected as President and Treasurer (no one else would take the office of Treasurer). Dr. Victor Alicea, President of Boricua College and former long-term Vice Chairman of the New York City Planning Commission, was elected Assistant Secretary. Alyah Horsford-Sidberry, a real estate professional and the granddaughter of one of the original Banana Kelly homesteaders, was elected Vice President and Assistant Treasurer. Mavelin Morales, a local homeowner and former social service director at Banana Kelly, was elected Vice President and Secretary.

I moved back to Kelly Street, living with my daughter and her family. While I worked in the field, Freddy Ferrer worked in the background and intervened directly when necessary. The rest of the board helped with governance.

Our concentrated efforts during that initial period simultaneously focused on saving and upgrading the buildings under our control through Housing Development Fund Companies (HDFCs); minimizing debt burdens of the various and sundry affiliated "paper companies" with nothing but debt on their books, and managing some very difficult outside relationships.

The Banana Kelly HDFCs. HDFCs are New York State low income housing corporations. Of the 23 buildings comprising the 16 HDFCs under Banana Kelly control (an HDFC can own multiple buildings), one building was vacant due to serious structural problems. Three buildings were in foreclosure by their respective mortgagees. Eight buildings were in federal bankruptcy court.

All 23 buildings were in poor physical condition. Many had serious problems with crime, particularly drugs. Most entrance doors had been broken, leaving the buildings open to outsiders. Similarly, most of the roof doors were broken, providing access to criminal elements. On a tour of the buildings in January and February 2003, we found that more that half of the apartments were being heated with kitchen stoves, and many had serious mold problems. All the buildings were encumbered by mountains of debt—about $4 million overall. We set to work repairing the physical and the fiscal problems. It was a mammoth job.

Ultimately, all the buildings in foreclosure were redeemed; the bankruptcy proceedings were dismissed; the tax foreclosure actions were abandoned. By the end of 2004, all the buildings had closed on refinance and renovation loans totaling over $45 million. By mid-January, 2005 all of the HDFC vendors had been paid.

Banana Kelly Community Improvement Association, Inc. This is the sponsoring entity that controls all the HDFCs and also contracts with the government for development and social services funding. In 2002, it owed about $400,000 in unpaid withholding taxes to the IRS.

After immediate lay-offs of all but critical staff, the organization was left with just seven workers, a sad remnant of an organization that had employed over 100 full time employees as recently as 1997.

In 2003, not a week went by without my learning about another lawsuit, default judgment or a new Notice of Levy. At one point, I made the somber recommendation to the board that we place the organization into bankruptcy and create a new organization with the sole purpose of overseeing the redevelopment and operations of the HDFCs. But the board Chairman, Fernando Ferrer, was adamantly opposed to that course of action. He had made a public commitment to those who were deceived and were legitimately owed funds, and he felt that every possible effort would be made to compensate all legitimate vendors. We struggled on.

Besides the debts, there were compliance issues. The last audited financial statements were from 1999. We hired an auditor to do three years' worth of financial statements. He stalled after 2000, and we hired Banana Kelly's first outside accountant from the late-seventies, Barry Milberg, to oversee completion of the rest of the audit work. Soon, we brought our annual reporting to the IRS and other government agencies up to date.

By the Fall of 2003, about one year after having assumed control, we were able to hire a new Executive Director, a local resident with an architectural background and considerable development experience. We provided him with the support he needed to allow him to grow into the job, reestablish our outside contacts, engage in fundraising and build on our ever-improving relations with our tenants.

Other Banana Kelly Affiliated Entities. This category represented a very tricky aspect of the workout. There were many affiliated entities that were basically "paper companies" with nothing but debt on the balance sheets.

Banana Kelly, Inc. had a judgment for over $600,000 against it in favor of the New York State Insurance Fund (workers compensation premiums, plus interest). Banana Kelly Development Corporation owed hundreds of thousands of dollars in withholding taxes. Banana Kelly Management Corporation had also failed to pay nearly $100,000 in New York State withholding taxes. Ultimately we settled all these matters, at a fraction of the outstanding liability.

Beyond the seemingly overwhelming circumstances, there were other complications that arose from outside relations, particularly with two local groups.

Meeting with MOM. Very soon after the new board was installed in the fall of 2002, a group called Mothers on the Move, or "MOM," demanded a meeting with me and Freddy Ferrer. This group had some leverage over us because they had successfully organized a rent strike in many of the Banana Kelly buildings. Since I had a good relationship with the group, which included receiving a "Social Justice Award" from them, I wasn't worried. I went to the meeting on my own, anticipating a give-and-take discussion. I was well aware of the problems that had persisted for a long time and involved not only physical repairs but also disrespect and abuse of our tenants. These problems provided adequate bases for anger on the part of the tenants and I was fully prepared to receive a decade's worth of righteous indignation. What I was not prepared for was the format for the meeting.

When I entered the room, there were several poster-sized sheets of paper filled with demands hanging on the walls. Next to each demand was a space for "Yes" or "No." I was told that my responses had to be restricted to one of those options. Out of the 30 or so demands, I answered only a few in the affirmative.

One of the primary demands was that the Southeast Bronx Community Organization (SEBCO) be fired immediately. Other demands called for immediate repairs and rent abatements. The meeting set the tone for our antagonistic relationship over the next six months of the transition.

Relief came unexpectedly. There was an attempted coup by a lead organizer and an outside legal consultant who tried to take over MOM because, among other things, they were indignant about one of the co-directors being a white man. The coup was unsuccessful, but there was a shake up, and MOM returned to its primary role: working as tenants' advocates rather than as organizers trying to overthrow management and transform the structure of Banana Kelly overnight.

"Peace in the Valley." The most difficult third-party aspect of the transition was our relationship with SEBCO, a relationship that went back almost 30 years to a time when Banana Kelly's volunteer efforts were just beginning in the shadows of SEBCO's multi-million dollar Section 8 development projects.

In the year 2000, Yolanda Rivera had entered into a contract with SEBCO to manage the Banana Kelly properties. The arrangement was very interesting. SEBCO had total control over property management operations; there was no provision for termination except in the event of bankruptcy, and the management fee was a whopping 12% of gross rental income. However, a year after the contract was signed, Yolanda terminated SEBCO, fired all of the union employees, and started a new management company, which she controlled.

SEBCO did not take this lying down. They went to court seeking an injunction, a remedy that is almost never granted in such situations. Nonetheless, SEBCO succeeded in obtaining a preliminary injunction. After that, the situation deteriorated, with even less attention being paid to building services. Tenants either paid no rent at all or paid rent to whomever they chose – SEBCO, Yolanda, or Mothers on the Move.

In November of 2002, the board had to pursue or settle the lawsuit against SEBCO. Based primarily on the enormity of other tasks confronting Banana Kelly, Fernando Ferrer opted for continuity and "peace in the valley." The board reinstated SEBCO.

But "peace in the valley" was not to last long. For about six months, I did try to make the relationship work, meeting once a week with SEBCO's Executive Vice President and taking a personal role in property management oversight and operations. But over time, the problems with SEBCO increased. There were disagreements over resident relations, housing court actions, union employees, the union itself, city regulatory agreements, rent security deposits, state and city registration requirements, and unauthorized disbursements to related third parties for questionable legal fees.

Father Gigante. SEBCO's Chairman was Father Gigante. I first became acquainted with Father Gigante when I worked at Casita Maria Settlement House in the early to mid-seventies. Even back then, the man was already a local legend. The youngest of his siblings, Louis Gigante grew up in Greenwich Village, did well in school, and had a very successful collegiate basketball career at Georgetown. After graduation, he went to seminary and afterwards spent some time in Puerto Rico before arriving at the St. Athanasius Parish in the early 1960s.

Gigante's brother, Vincent "Chin" Gigante, was the head of the Genovese crime family, so Father Gigante was sometimes reputed to be a "mob priest." Nonetheless, he became one of the most successful community developers of the 20th Century. In 1968, Gigante formed SEBCO – the Southeast Bronx Community Organization – and the organization went on to develop over 5,000 units of affordable housing in the Hunts Point-Longwood community. He also made two successful runs and served five years on the New York City Council.

In October, 1979, Father Gigante was sentenced to 10 days for contempt of court for invoking the priest-penitent privilege when called before a grand jury. I will never forget the scene at St. Athanasius Church when he was released three days early and was mobbed by thousands of adoring fans greeting their returning hero and savior. In short, "Father G," as he is known locally, was a local icon and institution in the South Bronx.

Yet Father Gigante is no hero of mine. Although it is difficult not to be impressed with his development record, his political savvy, and his overall success, that "success" represents much of what is wrong with community development today. Father Gigante is a very successful housing developer, but his success is entirely built on his charisma, his political connections, and his personal chutzpa. He has done little to enable any sense of "community" or even to ensure SEBCO's ongoing viability as a vital local institution in his absence.

In 2003, when it became obvious to Father Gigante that the relationship between SEBCO and Banana Kelly was doomed and that there was a diminishing chance that the buildings would fail (which would have given SEBCO the opportunity to take complete control), he offered to buy us out. The board refused, leading to the buy-out of SEBCO's contract in May of 2004. Property management was then turned over to Schur Management, a property management company originally brought in by Freddy Ferrer to assist Banana Kelly with property management and construction oversight.

By then, with most of the critical issues resolved, we believed that we were on our way to a new and improved chapter in Banana Kelly's history. But the struggle continued. By the Summer of 2006, it was it clear that our new Executive Director was not working out.

Back on Track. Banana Kelly lost nearly $270,000 from operations in 2005. By the end of June, 2006, the organization showed a net operating loss of about $110,000. With no effective construction oversight, the HDFC renovation schedule was two years behind; there were extensive cost overruns and other problems. There also was general resident dissatisfaction with services – this time directed at Schur Management. The Residents Council was disbanded and there were no active tenant associations in the HDFCs.

In August of 2006 the Board fired the Executive Director and once again took over direct control of operations. With intensified board oversight, including direct involvement in operations and an infusion of competent consulting services, Banana Kelly was on track once again.

By December 2006, the organization had a deficit of less than $30,000. A balanced budget for 2007 was put into place. With enhanced construction oversight, property management oversight, and asset management services, we received additional funds to complete the renovation of the HDFCs and expedite the conversion from construction to permanent financing.

Resident complaints subsided and our tenants once again began to cooperate and participate. Two resident leaders, Vera Roman of 788 Fox Street and Deirdre Wellington of 1290 Hoe Avenue, were brought onto the board of directors. The Residents Council was re-instated and began meeting regularly. And by early in 2007, the agenda for the meetings expanded beyond construction progress and property management to include social events to increase the participation of building and neighborhood residents in the organization. A special

Mother's Day event brought out scores of residents who shared home cooked meals, poetry readings, and aspirations with neighbors and friends. On July 14th, the Residents Council sponsored a Family Day and 30th anniversary celebration at Crotona Park in which about 100 residents, friends and neighbors participated.

Much of this success was due to the organizing efforts of Banana Kelly's Resident Organizer (and tenant), Hope Burgess. The changes taking place in 2007 also resulted from new leadership. Vera Rosario, a former area resident and with a professional background in supportive housing, took control as the new Executive Director in March of 2007. Since that time, she has coalesced the staff into a united and cooperative unit with a collective attitude of "service to the residents and community first and foremost." She has instituted an open door policy with residents; participated directly in construction and property management operations; begun to re-establish our links to the philanthropic community, and has successfully initiated the process that will return to Banana Kelly the tax credit properties removed from the organization's control some ten years earlier.

With the full support of the board, a solid base of committed residents with whom to work, a good staff, and a number of qualified outside consultants, the residents of Banana Kelly can once again call this organization their own. They feel the pride and purpose that only comes from active participation, the sharing of resources, and mutual cooperation – in short, the building of community.

XV The Loss of Community and the Loss of Democracy

Among many of my progressive friends and associates, "community" is a suspect concept. To them, community connotes small minds, nosy neighbors, interference with personal freedoms, intrusions into lifestyles, exclusivity, rigid conservative values, outright hypocrisy, hostility to outsiders, and resentment towards change.

Further, many of my associates are unhappy with the "sloppiness" that comes with true community – and popular democracy, for that matter. Outcomes are seldom predictable. Human variables are endless and constantly in flux. Self-interest often seems a predicate to voluntary participation in community processes, and irrationality appears pervasive.

Also, it takes a long time to get anything done.

But when asked for an alternative, these friends often seek social, economic and political systems that are like the systems presently in place, only with the "right" people in charge. That is, they, like most others, accept the status quo as immutable and essentially pre-ordained, but know in their hearts and minds that there is plenty of room within the system to better allocate benefits and burdens among its people.

I would maintain that this thinking is basically flawed because the future is not predetermined: the choices we make will determine what the future looks like. And in the absence of organized efforts against currently prevailing trends, we are heading towards a society where the individual will be powerless to participate in making political choices. Our democracy will ultimately transform itself into a system of government-sponsored free market capitalism with political power concentrated in the hands of the few and with all our political processes and institutions organized for the protection of the powerful. This trend is directly related to the loss of community in this country – a loss that should cause concern, but for the moment does not even generate recognition.

Community in Danger. Today, community as a social, political, and economic construct is gravely threatened. In its place, we have people isolated into individual household units and grouped into geographical clusters whose inhabitants are linked through infrastructure, and an organized system for the delivery of local services – water, schools, roads, and retail services. Further, these groupings – we generally call them neighborhoods – are totally dependent upon outside economic operations beyond the individual or collective control of those in the neighborhoods.

In the political realm, this transformation of communities into mere neighborhoods operating as externally-dependent, locally-serviced residential clusters has mirrored the transformation of citizens (active participants in the political life of society) into taxpayers and consumers of public services. This process of going from communitarian to consumer and from citizen to taxpayer is a direct function of the dominant economic system, which thrives on individual consumption patterns, workers who are detached from the resources needed for production, and citizens who are politically neutered and amenable to manipulation.

Why is this happening? It is happening because there is an inextricable link between an operating economy and political power. In the absence of local economy, there can be no local community. In the absence of community, there is no interdependence and no collective capacity. Without collective capacity there is no real political capacity. Without any political capacity in the hands of the ordinary citizen, there is no democracy. In its place, we have free market capitalism, which is increasingly being equated with (and which we are being conditioned to equate with) democracy.

Politics and Economics. In response to one outward manifestation of this process, namely "voter apathy," many choose to encourage activities that foster greater participation in the election process, such as sponsoring voter registration drives. But the only way to change a political system is to change the economic system. There are only two ways of doing that. You can work for massive, popular change of the economy from the inside. But how could such a thing ever occur? How could people transform the economy from within the current system? Could there be corporate reform through shareholders voting their shares in blocks large enough to change some of the basic motivations of corporate operations? Only the most ardent neoconservative optimist would follow this path. Alternatively, instead of attempting to reform the economy from the inside out, one could seek to supplant it from the bottom up, slowly and incrementally, by introducing local perspectives and local economic processes, such as the farmers' markets, that begin to disturb and even reverse the current dynamics, while at the same time rebuilding community.

Community Today: a Valid Social Construct? I have worked my entire adult life promoting community, but I will be the first to admit that community may no longer be a valid social construct. There may be little room for community in this global political economy, where society values consumption, mobility, and the concentration of wealth, and where the rewards of society are geared towards individual achievement. We must guard against what Karl Mannheim refers to as taking "flight into the security of a dead past."[93] Those engaged in community work must recognize that when they organize to "build community," they are also organizing against massive, overarching trends of society and the global economy. However, I know of no other form of viable social or-

---

[93] Karl Mannheim, *Ideology and Utopia, Collected Works of Karl Mannheim*, Routledge, 1998, p. 96.

ganization that can take the place of community within a popular democracy. Community allows people a voice and some element of control over their lives.

As discussed earlier in this book, community is a group of people joined by common circumstances (and/or interests, concerns, history, values, beliefs), having a degree of interdependence, and possessing the collective capacity to accomplish common goals. Developing community is a problematic endeavor because community is a problematic concept within the current political and economic system. It is just plain hard to fit the concept of community into prevailing social constructs, regardless of the intense nostalgia and affection with which the term is thrown about in academic, political, media and policy circles.

If we are to build community, we must contend with the forces that are working against community: individual isolation, economic marginality, and political disenfranchisement. These three manifestations are interrelated and cannot be dealt with effectively except as a whole.

Isolation is individualism taken to the extreme, and it is anathema to community. It is also the greatest threat to democracy.

In the workplace, we are overwhelmed by the ever-increasing demands of an information-based economy. Each of us is becoming less significant in relation to productive outcomes, and work is consuming more of our available time. Paradoxically, the more globally connected we become, the more isolated and vulnerable we will be as the importance of actual community decreases. Global communities cannot replace actual communities. It is similar to the difference between engaging in an amateur sports team, where all participants are engaged and interdependent, and being an individual minority shareholder in a large corporation, where each such shareholder is a necessary component of a massive, interconnected production machine, but where each investor is easily replaced, readily dispensable, basically anonymous, and in no way dependent upon any other investor.

Private People. As we have less time for leisurely pursuits, and as even our "free" time is to a large extent taken up with residual work activities (travel, reading, training, etc.), whatever downtime we have is being spent in efficient and isolated activities: online shopping, online entertainment, video games, private music and movie downloads. Such activities are efficient because they take very little, if any, planning; they can be interrupted and restarted seamlessly; and they are nearly always and everywhere available. These forms of isolated, atomized leisure activities fit well with the pervasive demands of our on-time, real-time, at-all-times global economy.

In this isolation, we may, perhaps, find contentment in the individual distractions that occupy our leisure time, but, in the process, we are becoming a nation of private people. All too readily we accept the contradiction inherent in being a "private citizen," just as we accept democracy as being represented by "free markets." It is worth recalling that in Ancient Greece, citizens who did not participate in the public realm were looked upon with disdain. The word "idiot" is derived from the Greek word *idiotes*, which means a person totally given to private interests. Ancient Greeks viewed such persons with scorn, even those who were successful at commerce.

Are we, then, fast becoming a nation of idiots? Given current trends, we are certainly at risk of becoming a nation of self-indulgent, narcissistic people, with no lives beyond work and raising a family.

Bowling Alone. In *Bowling Alone*,[94] a very influential book that examines how our social lives have diminished in recent years, Robert Putnam analyzes participation rates in social activities spanning many generations. He writes:

> Americans have been dropping out in droves, not merely in political life but from organized community life more generally.[95]

He discusses how our leisure activities focus increasingly on individual pursuit as opposed to collective pursuit.

---

[94] Robert D. Putnam, *Bowling Alone*, Simon & Schuster, 2000.
[95] *Ibid*, p. 64.

> The rise of electronic communications... has also rendered our leisure more private and passive. More and more of our time and money are spent on goods and services consumed individually, rather than those consumed collectively.[96]

Putnam goes on to provide prescriptions for addressing this loss of connectedness, and the concomitant loss of community and the social capital that goes with it. He compares this period of time to an earlier period a century ago when the economy was going through similarly traumatic transformations. Economic reorganization and immigration were turning us from a rural nation to a nation dominated by ever-growing industrialized cities. He cites the "reform movement" of the early twentieth century and how this redefined the public sphere within which politics operates, creating new and innovative institutions for involvement that led to the development of the most active and well-connected generation in our nation's history, the World War II generation. Putnam calls for a new dedication to civic enterprise and the creation of new institutional frameworks through which to involve people. And he criticizes those "idealists" who yearn for the past and try and re-create what is lost.

Putnam appears to be trapped by historical determinism, believing that the economic arrangements we have are inevitable and that it is nonsense to build any systems and structures contrary to the prevailing ones. But we do have the ability to make choices. We can work to build a future, to make history, if you will. The future is not predetermined unless we allow it to be.

Concomitant with the increase in individual isolation is the surrendering of public space. The more we isolate ourselves through the day's prevailing individualized distractions, the less time we have to meet, discuss, and engage with other members of society, let alone join with others in public action. We have become physically, socially, economically, and politically isolated.

Mobilization of Bias. As our isolation becomes more complete, general economic and political trends work against us in ways both direct and indirect. C. Wright Mills describes the process. Those in power do not necessarily make

---

[96] *Ibid*, p.243.

decisions with the intention of hurting any segment not in power, but over time, with decisions constantly being made to benefit one class of people or specific economic sectors, there is a "mobilization of bias" which not only harms those out of power but gives the appearance that the harm is part of an organized, thought-out plan. This is one of the reasons, I believe, that advocates are constantly being accused of being "conspiracy theorists." They see the seemingly organized and directed harm being done to particular groups and find it difficult to believe that it has come about without conscious and malicious intent.

This is a distressing state of affairs, leading to further despair. We feel unable to seek redress from our political institutions since they fundamentally respond to the economic organization of society, and those of us who are workers and consumers are not organized economically.

Selling off the Public Space. Isolation can be the midwife to fascism. As long we remain content with individual consumerism as a replacement for common interests, direct political engagement, and the collective pursuit of common goals, our heads remain in the sand and we do not even know enough to be scared that our liberties are being eroded.

In one of her many important works, Hannah Arendt posits that public space is a necessary precondition for a democratic society. She states that totalitarianism does not destroy freedoms or liberties, as such, but rather

> destroys the one essential prerequisite of all freedom which is simply the capacity of motion which cannot exist without space.[97]

This public space is the space within which citizens seek out the opportunity for individual and collective endeavors, engage one another, discuss the events of the day, ascertain the existence of common issues, arrive at common understandings of problems, and develop the approaches for addressing those problems. By its very nature, public space is a threat to a totalitarian regime and

---

[97] Hannah Arendt, *The Origins of Totalitarianism,* Harcourt Brace, 1976, p. 466.

must be destroyed or filled with some other all-consuming medium. In totalitarian societies, the replacing medium is propaganda, which instills a mixture of fear, suspicion, and paranoia. These occupy and preempt the public space that both joins and separates people and allows for all to be isolated, manipulated and made subject to the totalitarian regime.

What is public space? It is any space that allows people to interact. It does not have to be a formal meeting place, like meeting hall or public square. Public space can consist of a street corner, a laundromat, a bar, a café, a park bench, or even the internet.

Where is the public space today? I maintain that it is still fairly plentiful, but I worry that it is being voluntarily surrendered. In a totalitarian regime, public space must be expropriated. But the expropriation does not have be the result of government action. Our simple change in habits, whereby more of our entertainment has become personalized, ever-accessible, and pervasive, can subvert potential public space. In effect, we may be effectively selling public space to those who tender our private distractions to us.

Consumptive Voracity. And in this pursuit of personal gratification, which is only possible through the all-preemptive focus on earning money to survive and accumulating wealth (or debt), we lose our public spaces and our public selves. With consumptive voracity, we have allowed public relations, a trivialized news media, and distractive entertainment to become the new forms of propaganda. Instead of state propaganda, we have corporatist propaganda. Either way, the result is the same – we become isolated and vulnerable, even if those who wield power are benign.

In isolation, we are no longer truly free, and we are much more vulnerable to manipulation. Josef Goebbels, Hitler's propaganda minister, explained this process as one of "massification," whereby each person becomes an unthinking, isolated part of a giant industrial/military machine. This is accomplished once there is a transition from the private formation of public opinion to the public formation of private opinion.[98] I would argue that this process is occurring this very day, accelerated by the events of 9/11, which have added the threat to physical security to the economic insecurity felt by most Americans.

Today, American society is being converted into one manipulated, consuming mass. In Eastern Europe, after the fall of the Berlin Wall, the American democratic ideal was gleefully characterized and embraced by one man as, "canned beer and no responsibility." There is no need for public space if our lives become totally privatized and devoid of any sense of public duty. Public space is only necessary when people perceive the need and desire to pursue public action and public works. The loss of public space, the disinterest in its loss, just the same as the disinterest in the loss of community, represents a threat to our freedom and our democracy.

But What About the Internet? There are many who would argue that the internet, with its quick, easy access and global reach, is the new public space – the global agora, if you will. Are internet-based and internet-run organizations a new form of community? Can power derive from participation in these media?

No valid argument can trivialize the capacity and potential impact of internet-based activity. It can aid in the dissemination of information; it can raise money both near and far in ways unheard of even a decade ago; it can publicize a past occurrence to inform or embarrass or promote a future event to attract attention, attendance, and even to mobilize mass actions. It can reach millions in minutes, and power can be generated through its use. But that power is limited to making changes at the margins of our system and within the current set of power-sharing arrangements.

So even though the internet is a valuable tool, it is just a tool. Its use does not alter, create, or transform existing power-sharing arrangements, arrangements that derive from economic capacity and the political institutions built to protect, enhance and promote that capacity. The internet may help defeat a

---

[98] See *Power, Politics and People, The Collected Essays of C. Wright Mills,* Oxford University Press, 1963, p. 585.

candidate in an election. It may cause a public hearing to be postponed. It may temporarily influence corporate investment or production decisions. Occasionally, it may help oust a renegade politician or corporate official. But in the long run, it cannot replace community because it lacks one of the essential elements of community – interdependence. And the internet is unlikely to provide a solution to economic marginalization.

The New Revolution. Our economic marginalization goes hand in hand with our loss of community and loss of local political power. This economic marginality will not be overcome by higher voter participation rates, continual workforce preparation and re-training, election reform, campaign finance reform, term limits, and the like. We are in the midst of a new revolution – the technological/ informational/communications/genetic engineering revolution.

In the last revolution – the industrial revolution – tens of millions of Europeans were thrown off farms, amassed into cities, forced into poverty and otherwise denied the ability of making of a living. In Economics 101, many of us learned that these "displaced workers" of the 19th Century were simply re-trained and put back to work making and operating machines as part of the new industrial economy. However, this represents only part of the picture. At that time, whole continents were available for colonization. Entire peoples were eliminated by genocide or enslaved, and tens of millions of industrial revolution refugees from Europe could survive and thrive in the "New Worlds." Without this outlet and without the political and military machinery of colonialism to make it work, it is possible that the industrial revolution as we know it might have failed. Half of Europe was in the throes of revolutionary challenges in the mid-nineteenth century, which could well have ushered in socialist systems.

At present, there are no new colonies to establish. There is no place to which surplus labor can escape. Globally, there will continue to be massive population shifts, increased urbanization, increased prison populations, disease, war, famine and the like. In this country, the current trend toward globalized outsourcing is an attempt to ensure access to global resources and to rapidly and increasingly re-distribute wealth from the bottom 90% of the population to the top 10%. Of course, that redistribution is dependent upon the continued political apathy of United States workers, along with easy access to credit. Consumer debt keeps the population compliant and deluded as to its middle class status, while permitting transnational corporations to profit from ever-increasing consumerism at home while they pay lower wages abroad. But this can only be sustained for so long. Eventually, debt burdens will overcome the economic capacity of ordinary Americans, and there will be a major economic adjustment, resulting in a lowering of the standard of living for most Americans. The massive and sudden credit crunch of late 2007 may represent the first wave of this predictable trend.

Economic Marginalization. It is vital that people have access to the wealth generated by the local economy. Economic power is inextricably bound to political power. At the Bishop's Synod in Rome in 1971, the Peruvian delegation took the position that there can be no effective political participation without economic participation. They were saying that if you remove a group's ability to make a living then you destroy the very basis for its political involvement.

Economic marginalization occurs when people are totally dependent upon outside forces for their means of survival. This dependence permits us the luxury of isolation when our capacities have economic worth, but this very isolation becomes a curse if our particular talent is of no further use within the prevailing economy, or if the access point for the expression of that talent is simply removed (as through outsourcing). Without some way of making a living from within our local circumstances, we are economically marginalized. Without the local means for making a collective living (at least to some extent), we are politically disenfranchised as well. Power follows wealth, and if all wealth is generated outside our locality, then we have no effective control, no economy, no political power, and no community. As Wendell Berry cautions,

> The destruction of community begins when its economy is made... subject to a larger external economy... if you are dependent upon people who do not know you, who control the value of your necessities, you are not free and you are not safe.[99]

Our political disenfranchisement follows from our economic marginalization. Hannah Arendt points out how Hobbes predicted the concentration of political power as a necessary incident to the all encompassing goal of wealth acquisition as an end in itself.

> Hobbes was the true, though never fully recognized, philosopher of the bourgeoisie because he realized that acquisition of wealth conceived as a never-ending process can be guaranteed only by the seizure of political power, for the accumulating process must sooner or later force open all existing territorial limits. He foresaw that a society which had entered the path of never-ending accumulation had to engineer a dynamic political organization capable of a corresponding never-ending process of power generation.[100]

Political disenfranchisement must be seen as a function of the loss of local economic power. The further removed economic decisions are from people and localities, the more people become vulnerable and the more local politicians and political institutions become impotent. Political power follows wealth and wealth is going global.

As control of local resources – land, labor, capital, information, technology – has become further removed from localities, there has been a resultant diminution of local economic strength. With the loss of local economies, comes the loss of political power and the loss of community. Community has to have a foundation upon which to support collective endeavor. With the economic foundations undermined, local politics becomes a sterile exercise, and community is destroyed.

---

[99] Wendell Berry, *Sex, Economy, Freedom & Community*, Pantheon Books, 1993, pp.126, 128.
[100] Arendt, H., *The Origins of Totalitarianism*, Op. cit., p.146.

Developing Community. Any effort to build, rebuild, or develop community must take account of the three indispensable characteristics of community: commonality, interdependence, and capacity. The effort must address the prevailing manifestations of community loss: isolation, economic marginality, and political disenfranchisement. This is the challenge for anyone who takes the work of community development seriously.

But this challenge, as embodied in the chart below, is not adequately recognized within the community-building and social services sectors.

Attributes of Community	Destructive to Community
Commonality	Isolation
Interdependence	Political Disenfranchisement
Collective Capacity	Economic Marginality

If we are isolated, then we have nothing of political substance or real-world relevance in common with others. We may call a friend and agree about which "survivor" may be the next to be ousted from a popular so-called "reality show," but such a shared opinion is of no greater political moment than the caressing of a good book when the final chapter is read. There may seem to be a connection with the author, with the story, and with the characters, but the connection is pure fantasy.

Interdependence. Interdependence presumes political connections, since there is a perceived need for, and self-interest in, a system through which to productively engage others. How do we relate to one another? What are the rules of our mutual engagement? What redress is available when things go wrong? What processes and institutions are available to mediate our interactions? What resources are shared and which are private? How are such decisions made? How are challenges to be met – challenges that impact on an individual and on the community as a whole? Each of these questions has political implications. That is why interdependence presumes economic capacity and leads to political power.

In fact, we are all interdependent, and this interdependence is global in nature. The food we eat, the cars we drive, the fuel that heats our homes and provides electricity – these rarely derive from the local economy. The important issue for each of us is what economic, political and social institutions are in place and how we relate to such institutions. The further removed these institutions are from us, the more politically disenfranchised we become. The more politically disenfranchised we become, the more vulnerable and powerless we will be.

Individuals should be more economically secure now than in any time in human history since their collective economic capacity (the sum total of their economic output per capita) is unprecedented in the history of the world. Yet we do not feel economically secure. Economic marginality arises when the individual contributing (or potentially contributing) to collective productive output has little or no connection to other workers and no control over the economic institutions that make decisions about production, the location of facilities, compensation, product lines, etc. Economic marginality is directly related to a loss of control over natural and human resources and the means of production. Collective capacity presumes some level of control over those things that allow for survival and prosperity.

Power to the Elite. In our current system, an individual can prosper through independent initiative. But that success is totally reliant upon fortuitous access and his or her continued competence and utility. When we are no longer productive, we are tossed aside. However, those at the top work in concert with others at executive levels of corporate governance and control to ensure that they will be taken care of even after their usefulness has been exhausted. It is a contract among elites. In effect, I will share in profits now while I am of use, and I will be taken care of when my utility ends, just as you hope to be taken care of when you are no longer as useful. So while such golden parachutes may seem counter-intuitive in a capitalist system, they actually reinforce the system, which amply rewards those at the apex.

Power, whether in a corporation, a union, a social movement, or a community, results when people enter into agreements with others through which each contributes something to accomplish some set of collective goals. For those living in isolation at the economic margins, the capacity to politically covenant for such collective economic gain is extremely limited. Given the present concentration of wealth in the U.S., it is not surprising that most of the power in our country is concentrated in those with the greatest capacity to politically contribute to their own continued economic well-being.

In light of this depressing assessment, what is the future of community? If there is continued concentration of wealth, monopolization of the means of production by a small number of large economic entities, domination of markets by small numbers of conglomerates, intensified massification of the consumer sector, and increasing isolation of individuals into social units no larger than the household, then there is little hope that community will survive in the long run.

Rebuilding Community. In the short run, however, it seems a worthwhile endeavor to work for community preservation wherever community does exist and to assist in its rebuilding where it can enable collective action. But where do we start? Perhaps the most useful way is to help people escape isolation. This is not easily achieved, given the demands that people have on their time. But through the provision of some common space conducive to human interaction, starting with something as basic as providing working adults with some community space to share concerns (while their children are cared for), can help convert what seem to be personal problems into public issues and can result in collective resolve towards addressing these concerns.

Helping people connect to each other lets them realize that their problems are shared. This often leads to discussions that name and examine the problem, thus removing the feeling of isolated personal failure and de-mystifying the matter (eliminating the habit of always blaming "them" for the problem).

If people with common, shared circumstances can begin to explore the collective means of providing mutual support, the process will often lead to both interdependence and some collective capacity, even if initially limited. It is a start. And political arrangements will begin to emerge, providing the rudiments of community. Increased participation in existing institutional and electoral processes can help reverse the prevailing dynamics that make each of us socially, economically, and politically expendable (except to the extent that we are of service to the dominant economy).

Ultimately, all of us working in the community sector must learn that we make our own history. Existing paradigms, like empires, are inevitably displaced by new paradigms and new economic, social, and political arrangements. No one knows exactly how current arrangements will play out, but in the near future, at least, community will retain its roles in preserving and promoting popular democracy and in keeping us connected to each other.

Bibliography

Abrams, Charles, *The City Is The Frontier*, New York: Harper & Row, 1965
Allport, Gordon, *The Nature of Prejudice,* Cambridge: Perseus Books, 1979
Arendt, Hannah:
- *The Origins of Totalitarianism,* New York: Harcourt Brace, 1976
- *On Revolution*, London: Penguin, 1990
- *The Human Condition,* Chicago: University of Chicago Press, 1998

Berlin, Isaiah, *The Crooked Timber of Humanity,* New York: Alfred A. Knopf, 1991
Berry, Wendell, *Sex, Economy, Freedom & Community*, New York: Pantheon Books, 1993
Boyte, Harry C., *The Backyard Revolution*, Philadelphia: Temple University Press, 1980
Brandes Gratz, Roberta, *The Living City: How America's Cities Are Being Revitalized by Thinking Small in a Big Way*, New York: John Wiley, 1994
Byrne, Rhonda, *The Secret*, New York: Atria Books/Beyond Words, 2006
Chomsky, Noam, *Keeping the Rabble in Line,* Monroe: Common Courage Press, 1994
DeYoung, Raymond, "Environmental Psychology," from D.E. Alexander and R.W. Fairbridge, Eds., *Encyclopedia of Environmental Science*, Norwell: Kluwer, 1999

Freire, Paulo:
- *Education for Critical Consciousness*, New York: Continuum International Publishing, 1973
- *Pedagogy of the Oppressed,* New York: Continuum Publishing Company, 1970, 1993

Gallagher, Winifred, *The Power of Place*, New York: Harper Collins, 1993

Gifford, Robert, *Environmental Psychology, Principles & Practices*, Needham Heights: Allyn & Bacon, 1997

Gladwell, Malcolm, *The Tipping Point*, New York: Little Brown, 2000

Grogan, Paul S. and Tony Proscio, *Comeback Cities*, Boulder: Westview Press, 2000

Halpern, Robert, *Rebuilding the Inner City,* New York: Columbia University Press, 1995

Hunter, Floyd, *Community Power Structure*, Chapel Hill: The University of North Carolina Press, 1953

Jacobs, Jane, *The Death and Life of Great American Cities*, New York: Vintage Books (Alfred A. Knoff, Inc. and Random House, Inc.) 1961

Jiler, John, *Sleeping with the Mayor: A True Story,* St. Paul: Hungry Mind Press, 1997

Leavitt, Jacqueline and Susan Saegert, *From Abandonment to Hope:Community Households in Harlem,* New York: Columbia University Press, 1990

Lowinson, J. et al, eds., *Comprehensive Textbook of Substance Abuse,* N.P.: Williams and Wilkins, 1992

Mannheim, Karl, *Ideology and Utopia, Collected Works of Karl Mannheim*, London: Routledge, 1998

Mills, C. Wright, *Power, Politics & People, The Collected Essays of C. Wright Mills,* Ed. Irving Louis Horowitz, London: Oxford University Press, 1963

Nancy, Jean-Luc, "Of Being-in-Common," from *Community At Loose Ends,* edited by the Miami Theory Collective, Minneapolis: University of Minnesota Press, 1991

Peirce, Neil R. and Carol F. Steinbach, *Corrective Capitalism, The Rise of America's Community Development Corporation,* New York: The Ford Foundation, 1987
Putnam, Robert D., *Bowling Alone,* New York: Simon & Schuster, 2000
Ricci, David, *Community Power and Democratic Theory: The Logic of Political Analysis,* New York: Random House, 1971
Saegert, Susan et al., *Social Capital and Poor Communities,* New York: Russell Sage Foundation Publications, 2001
Schumpeter, Joseph A., *Can Capitalism Survive?* New York: Harper & Row, 1978
Sclavi, Marianella:
- *La Signora Va Nel Bronx,* N.P.: La Vespe, 2000
- *An Italian Lady Goes to the Bronx,* Milan: IPOC Press, 2007

Taguieff, Pierre-Andre, *The Force of Prejudice, On Racism and Its Doubles,* Minneapolis: The University of Minnesota Press, 2001
Weber, Max, *The Protestant Work Ethic and the Spirit of Capitalism,* London: Routledge Classics, Taylor & Francis Group, 2001

Printed in the United States
109863LV00005B/1-108/P

*Graduate Student Participants—Coral Gables Conference 2001
Organized by Jean Peck Krisch

Dissertators: **Nominated by Professor:**

W.F. Shively, University of North Carolina   Paul Frampton
"Conformality and AdS/CFT"

Hisham Sati, University of Michigan   Michael J. Duff
"Quantum Discontinuity for Massive Gravity with a Cosmological Term."

Andrea Soddu, University of Virginia   Pham Q. Hung
"Rare K Decays in a Model of Quarks And Lepton Masses."

Hai Yi, Southern University   Ali R. Fazely
"Latest Results of The LSND Neutrino Oscillation Experiment"

Michael A. Barnett, Florida International University   Stephan L. Mintz
"The Reaction $\mu^- + p \rightarrow \Lambda + \nu\mu$ and the Contributions
of The Individual Form Factors to the Cross Section."

J. O. Dunn, University of North Carolina   Paul Frampton
"Studies of Quintessence"

* *"The new Behram N. Kursunoglu Prize of $500 will be awarded for the best research presentation in the Graduate Student Session."*

            Annotators: **Thomas W. Kephart & Freydoon Mansouri**

          Session Organizer: **Jean P. Krisch**

3:00 PM   Coffee Break

3:30 PM   **SESSION XII:**   **Experimental Evidence for Black Holes**

        Moderator: **Elliott Bloom,** SLAC/Stanford University

        Dissertators: **Lynn Cominsky,** Sonoma State University
"How X-ray Telescopes See Black Holes:
Past, Present and Future."

                           Eric Becklin, UCLA
"Evidence for A Massive Black Hole
at the Center of our Galaxy"

                           Ramesh Narayan, Harvard University
"Evidence for Black Hole Horizons"

        Annotator: **Jeffrey D. Scargle**

        Session Organizer: **Elliott Bloom**

5:30 PM: Session XII ends.

6:30 PM   WELCOMING COCKTAILS, FOUNTAINVIEW LOBBY
             Courtesy of Lago Mar Resort